Abba's Answers

30 stories of God's answers to prayer

compiled and edited by
DEBRA L. BUTTERFIELD

CR

ST JOSEPH, MISSOURI USA

Contents

My Heart's Desires

Linda Highman

"Delight yourself in the LORD, and he will give you the desires of your heart. Commit your way to the LORD; trust in him, and he will act." Psalm 37:4–5 ESV

*P*romise by promise, experience by experience we learn God's provident and surprising love. As a young college co-ed who had never had a date, I did not expect to see God's love expressed in my first romance. I sang in a college radio choir; lunch came right after rehearsal, and many of us choir girls ate together. Often, we were joined by a comical, non-threatening fellow with a sweet tenor voice. Over time, by ones and twos, the girls dropped away from the lunch bunch until there was just the tenor and me. After a year or two, I surprised myself by confessing to my best roommate, "I love him!" It was the first time I had ever said that about a man! Startled, I stopped for a few seconds of serious consideration, and then I confirmed the fact: "I love him!"

Immediately, questions began, and they persisted for the next two and a half years. How does he feel about me? What kind of a relationship do we really have? Is this what God *really* wants for me? Is this His best for me, His plan for me? The tension built by these questions distracted me from my studies and drove me to play the dating games that had always disgusted me. Yet through this time, I was grounded by my daily devotional time, a habit I began when I was eleven years old. The Christian university I attended reserved one room on each dormitory floor as the prayer room. It was available at all hours for any who needed a quiet place to pray and meditate.

I was there in that prayer room every morning on my knees, asking God for guidance. One day while reading Psalms, I was struck by Psalm 37:4: "Delight yourself in the LORD, and he will give you the desires of your heart" (ESV). In a moment I memorized it. However, at first, I thought it meant God would give me what I wanted. But what did I really want? Did I really want the boy? Was he really *the one?* I found myself praying, "Lord, I want to want what you want me to want." Gradually, I realized the true meaning of the verse. By putting God first in my life, making Him the center of my heart, He would put *His* desires there. God doesn't *fulfill* our desires just because we read His Word every day or attend a Bible study or go to church. Rather, He gives us the desires themselves, the ones He wants us to have so that we can accomplish the big plans He has for each of us.

So, as I learned to ask for God's desires to be mine and for His perfect will to be accomplished, the events of my romance played out on two tracks. On one hand, I gained confidence that the sweet tenor was the man meant for me. On the other, I found myself deeper in love with my Jesus. When I vowed love, loyalty, and honor to Ed, I was also promising commitment to the concept of covenant, my intention to follow the next verse in Psalm 37: "Commit your way to the LORD."

In Genesis 15 and 17, God made covenant with Abraham. He promised him myriad descendants. Certainly, through millennia God has kept that commitment because He truly is *the* Promise Keeper. As a reflection of that godly attribute, wedding vows are meant to be permanent. Sadly, they seldom are kept because mere humans make them. When my marriage was hit by serious storms, and I felt my wedding vows weaken and my once warm love grow cool, I refused to entertain thoughts of divorce even though the culture encouraged it and Christian friends would have supported it. I refused the idea because I was committed to the unpopular principle of commitment. The desire for that commitment did not originate in my human heart. It was one of the desires put there by the One who is totally committed to keeping His promise of placing His desires into my heart.

Ed and I have shared careers, life's disappointments, and God's abundant joys. The years and their many experiences have echoed with Psalm 37:4 and 5, truly the only way to want what *He* wants and to discover the warm wealth of His divine love.

Suggested Prayer Topics

*P*ray about wanting what God wants.

My Messes and God's Greatness

Barbara Gordon

"So do not fear, for I am with you; do not be dismayed, for I am your God. I will strengthen you and help you; I will uphold you with my righteous right hand." Isaiah 41:10 NIV

My forehead rested on my gloved hands that clutched the steering wheel. The only sound was the thump, thump, thump of my heartbeat. What now, heavenly Father? I've really made a mess of things! A million stars illuminated the cloudless sky. When the sun went down, it took the wind with it, leaving behind an eerie silence.

Only a mere two hours earlier, I had dismissed my class of third graders. "Zip up your coats and put on your gloves. No snowballs on your way to the buses either." Squealing, hooting, and yelling children had warmed my heart, though the thermometer screamed a temperature that was far below warm.

When the last child climbed the steps to the bus, I hurried up the stairs in the old brick building, rubbing my hands together. Cold crept in around the windows of the poorly insulated classroom. I glanced at the clock and crammed an assortment of ungraded papers into a bag. The university was only forty-five minutes away, but with snowy conditions and the shortened days of winter, I needed to allow plenty of time to drive to my night class.

As I headed for my car, a freezing blast of wind whipped the heavy front door from my gloved hands. I shook my head as I briefly considered calling my new husband for advice. He was at work and would tell me to do what I thought was best. After stomping as much snow as I could from my shoes, I jerked on the car door handle. Several attempts later, ice cracked and splintered onto the gravel as the car door flew open. "Thank you, Jesus," I whispered as I flopped onto the driver's seat.

The determination to make the trip was the first of several bad decisions that night. Snow and ice covered the roads and the temperatures plummeted. Poor route choices in the era before cell phones and modern means of clearing pavement, culminated in my being stranded on a narrow, deserted road.

After berating myself to God, I lifted my head and tried to estimate how far to the hazy glow of a light in the distance. Half mile, a mile? My shoes made a squeaky sound on the thin ice before sinking into the softer snow beneath. Chiding myself for the absence of snow boots, I was at least thankful for the warm coat, gloves, and scarf I'd donned that morning.

Thoughts tumbled through my mind. Should I try to follow the road? The shortest way would be through that pasture. Lord, if You are listening, help me scale that fence.

Snow crept up past my knees as I descended into the ditch. Please God, let that light beam belong to an occupied house. I took a deep breath and mentally encouraged myself. Ignoring the pain, stress, and elements of nature, I separated the ice-covered strands of barbed wire and stepped through the fence.

I was oblivious to time, trekking across the frozen earth. My eyes were glued to the far-off surreal glow of light, but my thoughts bounced from one notion to another. A deep yawn swallowed my face. I wonder if you really do become overwhelmed with sleepiness before freezing to death.

After what seemed like hours, my watch said twenty minutes had passed. I leaned in, placed a hand on one knee and breathed heavily. My gloved hand raked across my numb face and a shudder of chills raced down my spine. Pushing my shoulders back, I resumed my pace on the heavy wooden blocks that had been my feet.

A dance of light and shadows appeared. I placed my hands on the flutters in my belly and gazed up at the nearby yard light. The pungent smell of wood smoke directed my glance to the illuminated farmhouse. A jolt of hope coursed through my weary body.

"Come in, come in! Mama, come here, this lady needs help."

The farm couple scooted their chairs close to hear my trembling voice. The farmer offered a telephone, while his wife fetched a minty smelling cup of hot tea. I rocked back and forth under the heavy quilt my new friends provided. Wrapped around the warm teacup, my hands began to thaw and my eyes grew heavy.

The farmer gave good directions and a couple of hours later the doorbell aroused me from my near sleep state. Relief and my husband's strong arms engulfed my tired body.

God used a patient husband, a borrowed four-wheel-drive pickup, and a kind farmer's dependable tractor to demonstrate His unconditional love. My notion that God's provision depends on my actions was challenged on that cold night. I discovered His faithfulness is not contingent on me doing the right thing but is a result of His infinite love. Even when my predicament is the result of my own hasty and negligent behavior, He still loves me. This realization opened the door to an intimate relationship with God I had not imagined possible. God's greatness is bigger than all my messes.

"So do not fear, for I am with you; do not be dismayed, for I am your God. I will strengthen you and help you; I will uphold you with my righteous right hand" Isaiah 41:10 (NIV).

Suggested Prayer Topics

Thank God for those He places in our paths to teach us of His greatness. Pray for opportunities to tell others about His greatness.

Because We Love You

Barbara Villarreal

"The LORD your God in your midst, the Mighty One, will save; He will rejoice over you with gladness, He will quiet you with His love, He will rejoice over you with singing." Zephaniah 3:17 NKJV

The end of March rocked back and forth from sunshine to rain. My family battled allergies and sinus infections. Most of us were on the mend in time to enjoy the first long day of the season. A family gathering would be in order and soon.

Post-operative issues brought me to stay with my oldest daughter, Christina.

My other two daughters and my daughter-in-law decided to visit Christina's house as well. Out of my ten grandchildren, seven are under the age of three. They filled the house with laughter, play, and running in and out of the backyard throughout the day and evening. Family gatherings are a regular occurrence since Christina bought a big house that is centrally located between all of us. My son-in-law grilled several different meats and sides while the women wrangled children and talked about life.

Three-year-old Penelope delighted in testing her parents with a new-found freedom of going to play in the front yard. The backyard, complete with privacy fence and locked gate, was filled with slides, riding toys, and balls. It was a huge space by anyone's standards. The front yard consisted of a few flowers, a bit of grass, and a patch of dirt. It also, even though in the middle of a cul-de-sac, was the best view of Penny's expanding world. Anyone who knows how three-year-olds think would know the front would be her preferred play space.

Time with small children had taken its toll on my postoperative body. Cries filled the house, announcing the day needed to come to an end. All of the children, and possibly the mothers, were well past the point of exhaustion. Three-year-old Penny, with her two-year-old cousin in tow, put in a request to go to the front yard.

The parents tried to explain many times that the front yard was off limits unless an adult was free to keep an eye on them. Penny continued to push. The last time she asked, she was told no. Her next question, of course, was why. She is three. The answer was delivered in almost perfect unison at top volume. It was the patented parent answer from both her parents. "BECAUSE I SAID SO!"

Ouch. I think we all felt the pain the crushing statement delivered. Before a rebuttal could be made, as if on the air itself, a soft voice drifted amongst the chaos that announced the truth. "Because we love you."

My daughter-in-law Kaya did not give a thought to her own loving words as she walked Penny to the back door, lightly touched the child and gave her a Disney worthy smile that left the poor child with no defense. Penelope smiled back at her aunt and walked into the backyard without another moment of fuss.

From that moment on, the phrase "because we love you" stuck with me as if there were a nugget of meaning I was missing.

There was.

As parents, we can become tired and frustrated with our children and their daily conversations that normally have a multitude of whys located throughout. While they are repeating the same word over, we change our answer to go with each question asked. They hear a variance in our answers, even though all of our answers have the same meaning: I love you enough to take the anger you are directing toward me and remain firm in saying no.

The love we try to show our children is as lost on them as God's love is on us at times. The trick is to remember amid chaos and complaints that our main goal as parents is to keep our children safe while letting them know how much we love them. A child's constant barrage of questions hides the real question: "Do you love me?" A parent's reply always seems to hide the answer: "Yes, I will always love you."

God faces the same issues with His children when we ask why. Abba's answer is always, "Yes, I will always love you."

God confirms this in several passages but one of my favorites is Zephaniah 3:17: "The LORD your God in your midst, the Mighty One, will save; He will rejoice over you with gladness, He will quiet you with His love, He will rejoice over you with singing."

Suggested Prayer Topics

*P*ray for parents to have the patience needed as they raise their children. Pray to be more aware and open to how God displays His love for you.

The Compassion Story

Cathy Krafve

"Therefore, having been justified by faith, we have peace with God through our Lord Jesus Christ, through whom also we have access by faith into this grace in which we stand, and rejoice in hope of the glory of God." Romans 5:1–2 NKJV

We sat on the couch together, holding hands and looking into each other's eyes. How would he respond, with rejection, judgment, or condemnation? Was he going to regret marrying me? Would he want a divorce?

Up until that moment, I never said abortion out loud. The word had a magic power over me. Even years after the event, I felt like hiding, always ready to dodge the topic. When we fell in love, I didn't have the nerve to tell this wonderful man about my past. I devoted myself to living in the present without looking back. But it wasn't easy.

In the 1980s, every sermon seemed devoted to the wrongs of abortion. I knew lots of verses reminding me of God's love and forgiveness, like Romans 5:1–2. "Therefore, having been justified by faith, we have peace with God through our Lord Jesus Christ, through whom also we have access by faith into this grace in which we stand, and rejoice in hope of the glory of God" (NKJV).

My head knew I was supposed to trust God's grace to forgive myself, but my heart refused to believe.

Each Sunday, I sat in the pew, ready to run for the bathroom, feeling like I would vomit. I tried hard to forget, but I remembered the smell of the pungent cleanser they used at the clinic and the weird way the light bulbs reflected my anxiety.

After the abortion, I dramatically changed my lifestyle, determined to avoid repeating my mistake. I quit dating. Instead, I began building friendships. However, as David and I moved toward a serious relationship, my unspoken fears haunted me.

I owed him the truth. Yet, somehow, the conversation always evaporated before it started. How could I marry him when I could not tell him about my past? Intuitively, I believed David would forgive me for keeping such a secret. In my mind, I always call this the Compassion Story. Compassion is one reason I knew I could marry David.

About four years after we married, I began to have symptoms related to lingering abortion trauma, called Post Abortion Syndrome. Of course, I needed serious counseling. By then, I held two beautiful toddlers in my lap. But holding them was beginning to hurt my soul because of the baby I never held. Unspoken grief was robbing me of joy with my children.

Eventually, I sought help. After weeks of sitting on her couch, sobbing and struggling to forgive myself, my counselor spoke a truth into my life I will never forget.

"Cathy, I admire your courage."

No one had ever admired my courage before. Steadying my wounded soul, I searched deeply for the courage I needed for a life-changing conversation. Finally, the day came when I would tell David.

I held my breath for a moment, then exhaled and told him about my abortion. Instead of rejecting me, David tenderly wrapped his arms around me. Then he said the most loving words I believe I've ever heard.

"Cathy, I am so sorry you had to go through that."

Right then and there, my heart began to heal in its most sacred, yet wounded place. If this good man, the father of our young children, could forgive me and still cherish me, perhaps God truly loved me unconditionally as well. Was there ever better evidence of God's own mercy and grace toward me?

Grace is what God offers us while He waits for us to recognize our need for His mercy. We walk in our denial, working out our own plan for perfection. All the while, God has already prepared mercy, forgiveness, and redemption—a whole smorgasbord of refreshments designed to fuel us for companionship with Him. It's like an all-you-can-eat buffet of spiritual nourishment prepaid by Jesus' sacrificial death on the cross. Our value and instinctive self-worth are confirmed by His resurrection.

However, shame makes us want to hide in the bushes, like Adam and Even when God was looking for them after they disobeyed Him. Why do we hide? Shame tells us we are of no value; we can't face the rejection we deserve. Who could love us, knowing our failings and self-centeredness?

In order to come to the table, we have to believe He receives us, warts and all. Then, to keep receiving nourishment from Him, instead of hiding, we have to stand in His grace. Ah, to be so authentic that we never have to hide again! Standing in grace, being our vulnerable self no matter what anyone else thinks, trusting God to love us when everyone else may reject us, takes courage.

Yet, even in our most sinful, self-willed moments, God still reaches out to us and offers forgiveness in His Son. Jesus has already paid the full price for our most selfish decisions, our most independent sinful choices, if we will but receive His gift.

Finally, with my husband's tender encouragement, I am beginning to stand in grace. By faith I trust God to give me daily access to His grace, then I stand. Okay, sometimes I sit, crawl, or cry in His grace, too, just to be perfectly authentic. However, no matter the struggle to believe in His grace, there is a wonderful reward. His grace allows us to "rejoice in hope of the glory of God."

Yes, standing in grace takes courage. But when we do, God will appoint someone gracious and full of compassion, like my husband demonstrated, to confirm His love for us.

For your own dear heart:

1) Who epitomizes courage and compassion in your life?

2) How have you demonstrated God's unconditional love and patient grace to someone this week?

3) When you pray, how can you ask God for grace in a specific situation you face now?

Suggested Prayer Topics

A sk the Lord to help you have compassion for yourself and others. Pray for His courage in your life.

A Powerful Lesson

Linda Center

"Then Peter remembered the word Jesus had spoken: 'Before the rooster crows, you will disown me three times.' And he went outside and wept bitterly." Matthew 26:75 NIV

I once denied Jesus, the same way Peter denied Him. There was no rooster involved, but God used another woman to call me on my choice.

Recently, the facilitator of our local poetry club asked if I would give the invocation for their next meeting. Since most of my poems are inspirational, I assumed she thought I was a good choice to offer a prayer. For days, I pondered her request because she ended the conversation with, "Please be sensitive to those who hold different beliefs."

The morning of the meeting, I entered the country club feeling apprehensive about the words I should use. After they announced my name, I stepped behind the podium, reaching for the microphone. I spotted a man in the front row who had made a sarcastic comment about my poem "Living for God" at our last meeting. "It must be nice to have faith," he sneered.

"I count on my faith to get through the day."

"Sure you do. I don't want anything to do with a personified God," and he walked off.

Now, this same man glared at me while I asked the audience to bow their heads.

I cleared my throat and took a deep breath before I asked the Lord to fill the room with His presence and bless our time together, but I found myself cutting the blessing short. At the end of the prayer, I said, "We ask these things," and then I hesitated. In a split second, I chose not to say, "in Jesus' name." I ended the prayer with a simple "Amen."

Eyes lowered, I cringed back to my seat. I kept repeating the prayer in my mind and felt I had betrayed my Lord.

After the meeting, I hurried to the drink station for a glass of water. An elderly woman stopped me and softly asked, "May I talk to you, in private?"

"Yes, ma'am." I touched the back of her arm and led her to an empty corner.

She smiled. "I enjoyed your prayer, but I would have enjoyed it more if you had said in Jesus' name at the end."

I dropped my eyes, wishing the floor would swallow me whole. A second seemed forever, trying to find the right words. "Thank you for your boldness. I needed to hear that."

She hugged me and whispered, "One last thing—God knows your heart, and His love for you will never change."

I ran to the car, climbed in, and pounded the steering wheel. I asked for forgiveness and promised God I would never end a prayer again without using Jesus' name. I asked the Lord to give me another opportunity to pray in public. I sensed the presence of God. "My daughter, you failed the test, but you got the lesson. All is forgiven and forgotten."

The apostle Paul openly admits he was a prisoner of sin. He said in Romans 7:15, "I do not understand what I do. For what I want to do I do not do, but what I hate I do" (NIV). Paul had a problem with the desires of the flesh. He continually struggled between his desires and God's. People have not changed much since Paul's time. Fear is a problem most people have difficulties overcoming, including fear of what people think of us. Fear can alter our decisions, sometimes for good, sometimes for evil. God uses these struggles to test our commitment and for correction.

What happened to me at the luncheon was more than a test. It was a powerful lesson.

Has there been a time you had a chance to witness for Jesus and you made a choice not to? Were you in a place that it was uncomfortable to bring up Jesus' name?

Take heart. God's Spirit in our lives can change our speech and actions. Galatians 5:16 and 17 tell us, "So I say, walk by the Spirit, and you will not gratify the desires of the flesh. For the flesh desires what is contrary to the Spirit, and the Spirit what is contrary to the flesh. They are in conflict with each other, so that you are not to do whatever you want" (NIV). When the Spirit leads us, we draw on His strength, rather than our own, to resist temptations. Because of Jesus, we have victory over life's struggles. God refines us as silver is refined, polishing us to be more like Him.

Suggested Prayer Topics

Thank the Holy Spirit for His guidance in your life. Ask Him to provide His strength to be a bold witness for God.

God Waits to Bless Us

Jeanetta Chrystie

"Now to him who is able to do immeasurably more than all we ask or imagine, according to his power that is at work within us, to him be glory … for ever and ever!" Eph. 3:20–21 NIV

I felt sheepish asking God to show me in a tangible way whether I was to consider dating any of the men who invited me on a first date. However, dating after age forty can be awkward at best. Since my church did not have a singles ministry, I decided, in my own wisdom, to attend singles events at a few churches around town. But I didn't feel comfortable accepting dates with men I barely knew, especially if they wanted to find out where I lived and pick me up.

So, I decided to counter with the idea of a lunch date. I offered to meet at an eatery where I at least knew I liked the food—and some of the waitstaff knew me. If a man hesitated, I'd suggest coffee on Saturday. If he refused both, I politely rejected his offer of any type of date.

After a few workday lunches or Saturday coffee dates, if a

man seemed nice and I learned more about his church life and Christian walk, I might allow meeting at a daytime venue such as the zoo or event at his church. Still, I was too uncomfortable to let a man pick me up at my home and ride in his car.

Also, I desired a real relationship, one that could grow into something more. Slowly I realized my wisdom was lacking. I needed to ask God for His help and guidance.

I asked God to show me whether I should date a man beyond the first date by having the man bring something "girly" for me, such as a flower or stuffed doll. My sheepish feeling continued when I remembered the Bible story of Gideon who "put out a fleece" to confirm God's direction.

Gradually, I forgot about my fleece and began accepting second and third dates until I discovered each man and I were not a well-suited match. I listened to many men complain about their ex-wives, and a few lament about a deceased wife with too many details about why and how she died. More than once a man proposed marriage after less than four dates. Two men proposed on our first date! One was obviously still in love with his first wife who had divorced him. The other suddenly showed me a picture of his previously unmentioned six children, ages one to sixteen. He didn't want a wife; he wanted a caregiver so he could focus on his very important job. I quit dating.

"God, I guess I'll have to trip over him if you want me to date anyone," I said.

Several months later, a heavy snowfall encouraged me to walk to a corner church instead of driving to my downtown church. I met the elderly pastor and his wife, enjoyed an uplifting worship service, and they insisted I join them in their home for lunch. After explaining why I visited their little church, I gave in at Ted and Martha's urging and joined them for spaghetti and meatballs.

We became friends. They learned my dad was also a pastor. I learned an encouraging story about how they met in later life as widow and widower.

Then I remembered my fleece. Upon returning to my townhome, I renewed my request with God, but I still didn't want to accept any more dates.

This sick-of-dating attitude probably limits God, I thought.

But God showed me His surprising and unlimited love. Ted's son planned an eight-day visit for his dad's birthday.

"His flight arrives well after dark," said Ted. "Would you mind picking Keith up at the airport and bringing him to our house?"

How could I refuse this sweet couple? Soon, late one Friday night, I met Ted's son at the airport.

God was ready to set goosebumps on my skin. Keith arrived with a suitcase in one hand. His other hand held a silk rose with an attached five-inch stuffed panda. I caught my breath as I accepted the surprise gift. Was God answering my fleece? Was I supposed to consider a relationship with this preacher's son from 2000 miles away? God seemed to be making sure I didn't miss the clue by giving Keith the idea to buy both a rose and a panda doll for me in the Seattle airport.

I allowed this stranger into my car and drove back across town to drop him off at his dad's house. When we arrived, Ted grabbed Keith's suitcase at the door and shooed us off into the night.

"We've already eaten supper. Would you take my son to your favorite restaurant to eat?"

Four hours later, Keith and I continued to talk beyond the restaurant's closing time. We had so much in common and spent every evening together for the next eight days. When it was time for Keith to catch his return flight, we agreed to email regularly. (This was before free long-distance cell phone calls.) Thousands of long, daily emails and many airplane flights later, Keith proposed marriage. This time I accepted the proposal, and God has richly blessed our lives for many years.

God had a plan all the time. He waited for me to quit following my own wisdom, ask Him for help, and give Him free rein in my love life. As Ephesians 3:20–21 says, God proved to me that His plans are bigger and better than I could ask or even imagine.

I could never have planned a snowfall to send me to a neighborhood church to meet a couple with a son who was searching for a committed Christian wife as I was searching for a Christian husband who would treasure me as precious. God loves to amaze us. We only need to let Him.

Suggested Prayer Topics

Ask God to reveal any area in your life where you might be following your own wisdom. Then commit to trust Him instead.

Be Still, Pray and Wait

Carolyn Fisher

"He says, 'Be still, and know that I am God; I will be exalted among the nations, I will be exalted in the earth.'" Psalm 46:10 NIV

Going through a separation was the worst thing that ever happened to me. However, now fifty-seven years later I can say it was the best thing that ever happened. My husband and I were married very young, and after eighteen years, he came home one morning and said he didn't love me, never had loved me, and was leaving. Two weeks later I found out it was because he believed the grass was greener on the other side. I refused to play the game and told him if he wanted a divorce, he would have to get it. I continued to pray and seek others to pray with me.

One morning, he was to meet me at our seven-year-old daughter's school. He would take her to the fall festival and then out to supper. We drove into the school lot at the same time. He walked to the car to get her and they walked away.

My daughter looked back to wave goodbye to me. At that moment, a wave of loneliness, abandonment, and feeling of being unloved swept over me. Uncontrollable tears came, and I couldn't understand why I was feeling that way.

As a child growing up, I assumed I would go to heaven because I went to church and was a good girl. My parents always went to church, taking me with them. But when I was ten, my Sunday School teacher took our girl's class to a tent revival in the town where we lived. When one of my friends went forward, I followed her. That day, I accepted Jesus as my Savior and was baptized a few weeks later in our church.

My dad was military, and we moved all the time, never settling anywhere for very long. It was hard to get involved in things because of that. Due to all the moving, I was never discipled in my new decision to follow Jesus.

When I met my husband, he was in the military as well, but had come from a very active Christian family. When my parents met him, they said, "Don't bring anymore home; he's the one." They loved him. He was a wonderful young man, didn't drink or smoke, and went to church. He discovered Jesus at a church camp. When his best friend went forward, he followed him. So, in looking back, I think our decision for Jesus was due to peer pressure for both of us.

That day in the parking lot of my daughter's school, after all the tears, it suddenly occurred to me I wasn't alone or abandoned, because Jesus loved me. I was a sinner saved by grace, and He still loved me. Because of being single, I was lonely and had pulled away and wasn't studying His Word or involved in a good church. I was talking the talk but not walking the walk. I was pretending and playing at being a Christian. That morning after asking Jesus into my heart again, and this time meaning it, things changed inside and out. After a lot of tears and realization of where I was in life, this new commitment to Jesus made all the difference. I got into the Word and also began reading some books on mid-life crisis to understand what my husband was going through. I joined prayer groups and fellowship groups, trying to learn anything I could.

It was a very painful two and a half years. But God was teaching me to depend on Him. I was a little stubborn and tried to get ahead of Him, but I finally learned who was in charge, and if I would be still and know He was in charge, things would progress much more quickly. I guess I'm a slow learner because I kept wanting to help Him out and He would put me in my place.

During this time, there were changes in my husband as well, and even though it took so long, it was worth every minute. God answered my prayers, returned my husband as a new man, and we went on to celebrate almost fifty-four years. I will be forever grateful to my Lord and Savior.

We moved across the States so we wouldn't have everyone giving us their two cents. We wanted to depend only on God, so we packed up a big yellow truck, and with my parents in tears, we drove off from Orlando to Seattle. Our oldest had just graduated and didn't want to go, so she stayed behind, getting married two years later while we were away. Our eight-year-old was excited because her mommy and daddy were back together. We knew in our hearts this was what God was telling us.

Three years later, God brought us back to Florida to help care for our aging parents. During those years away, we had to learn to pray together, be still, and wait on God. Those are not easy things to do, but God is a big God and He can take care of it. And He did!

"Now faith is the substance of things hoped for, the evidence of things not seen" (Hebrews 11:1 NKJV).

Suggested Prayer Topics

*P*ray for those who are battling strained relationships. Pray for prodigals to return.

All My Broken Pieces

Norma C. Mezoe

"And we know that in all things God works for the good of those who love him, who have been called according to his purpose." Romans 8:28 NIV

I paced across the parsonage kitchen, pausing occasionally to look out the window. Across the wide parking lot, I could see people wandering around outside the church.

Earlier that night, Mike, my husband, who was in his first full-time position as a minister, had attended a deacon's meeting, which lasted until eleven. He came home, sat at the kitchen table, and said, "I have some thinking to do." Then he left the house.

When the clock struck midnight, he still hadn't returned. Anxious to know what was happening, I phoned the wife of one of the deacons. "Mary, can you tell me what's going on?" Mary hesitated, then told me that Mike had run off with a young mother from the congregation. I had not known of their affair, and I felt as though I were a glass thrown on concrete. The pieces of my life lay shattered around me.

I waited alone through the night, watching for my husband to return. But even though I was physically alone, I wasn't alone. I could feel God's presence giving me a serenity that could have come only from Him.

Morning dawned and a new day began. Mike returned and told me he was leaving me for the other woman. He hurriedly grabbed some of his clothing and walked out of my life.

Even though I had never worked outside my home, I realized I had no other choice. I had to find a job. But what could I do? I had only a high school education and no work skills in the business world. To compound that problem, I didn't have transportation. Mike had taken our only car.

But God was working. He had a plan for my life; all I needed to do was trust Him.

The night Mike left, I began claiming the promise of Romans 8:28: "And we know that in all things God works for the good of those who love him, who have been called according to his purpose."

Soon, I learned of a temporary job that would be for one month at minimum wage. I applied for and received the employment. There was still one big problem: lack of transportation! The job was thirty-five miles away. The day before my work began, I was given a used car, complete with license and insurance.

I had worked at my job of telephone recruiting for one week when the secretary of that nonprofit organization quit. She recommended me for the position, and the next morning I was interviewed.

On my resume, the first I had ever submitted, I listed skills gathered as a mother and as the wife of a minister. Despite my lack of higher education or work experience, I was hired. My position began that day.

The Bible tells us to pray without ceasing (1 Thessalonians

5:17). I found myself doing that. Our office served seven counties, and there was a wide variety of things I needed to learn. It was a two-person office and at the time I was hired, there wasn't a supervisor. The secretary I was replacing was supposed to stay on for a week to train me, but after two days, she left. A volunteer helped me learn many of my duties. I worked alone in the office until a supervisor was hired three weeks later.

The organization was one that helped cancer patients. During my six years there, I was able to give comfort and guidance to many patients and their families. Sometimes I arranged transportation so patients would be able to go to their treatment centers. Other times, I gave encouragement through listening and letting the patients and families know that someone cared.

A few years after my husband left, I became a published writer. After an article about my husband's leaving was published in a national magazine, I received letters and phone calls from people across the United States. Many of these had also been abandoned by a spouse; all of them had problems and heartaches. As I talked with and wrote to these hurting men and women, I prayed, asking God to guide me in my thoughts and words. Just as God gave hope to me, He used my writing to bring hope and encouragement to others.

Through the years since my husband left, there have been other problems and heartaches, but God has been there for me, working in them for my good.

The trials have helped me to grow spiritually, and I've learned to depend more fully upon His guidance. Through all the bumps I've encountered in my life and continue to face, I have learned that no problem is too big for God.

It has been thirty-six years since God lovingly gathered all my broken pieces and wove Romans 8:28 through my life to give me a new beginning.

Suggested Prayer Topics

Pray for people going through divorce.

Names have been changed to protect privacy.

I Will Praise Him for the Victories

Debra L. Butterfield

"Why am I discouraged? Why is my heart so sad? I will put my hope in God! I will praise him again— my Savior and my God!" Psalm 42:11 NLT

There was a time in my life when, like Narnia frozen in 100 years of winter, my life felt shrouded in perpetual darkness. We've all been there, that place where life is in crisis mode and our prayers bounce back from the ceiling. I wondered, "Why is this happening to me?" and "When is it going to end?"

I was tempted many times to turn away from God, but the thought of eternity in hell prodded me to hold on. It took nearly ten years before the darkness melted away. My faith in God took a terrible beating. I often tempered my prayers with "God, help my unbelief" (Mark 9:24).

I spent a lot of time reading the Bible. Whenever I read Exodus and God's deliverance of the Israelites, I would wonder why they complained so much. They spent forty years in the desert with selective amnesia, forgetting how God mightily delivered them from the Egyptians through ten miracles. He parted the Red Sea, poured water from a rock, and rained down manna from heaven as they journeyed to the Promised Land.

I used to think if I witnessed those kinds of miracles, I'd have unshakable faith in God. I would ask God why couldn't He do amazing things like that in my life and fix everything that was wrong?

I asked Him to help me understand the Israelites' attitude.

I began to read five psalms every day. I witnessed David crying out to God, proclaiming his troubles and being nitty-gritty honest with how he felt about it all. David's example in the Psalms taught me to pour out my heart to God.

God also showed me David eventually turned to praise. When he got discouraged, he encouraged himself by recalling past victories God brought him through. "I will praise you, LORD, with all my heart; I will tell of all the marvelous things you have done" (Psalm 9:1 NLT). "The LORD who rescued me from the claws of the lion and the bear will rescue me from this Philistine!" (1 Samuel 17:37, NLT).

In all my "Why this? Why that?" God showed me I was just like those Israelites. Perpetually complaining, but never remembering or praising Him for all the answered prayers. Throughout my adult life I have had a tendency...no, a habit of focusing on the negative things in my life. I didn't see my victories because I focused on the defeats.

Negative memories overpowered the positive. When in the midst of crisis, recalling previous victories can be difficult. The current grueling circumstances can overwhelm us. But God brings us the same answer He gave the Israelites. "After the victory, the LORD instructed Moses, 'Write this down on a scroll as a permanent reminder" (Exodus 17:14a NLT). A memorial such as this reminded the Israelites of their victories, of God's promises to them, and of God's faithfulness to fulfill his promises. God often commanded the Israelites to build memorials as well.

My habit of focusing on the negative kept the shroud of darkness in place much longer than it might have otherwise been. When God seemed more distant than the stars, He taught me to encourage myself through the dry and difficult times by remembering all the answered prayers and victories He had already brought me through.

Now I cultivate a habit of focusing on the victories rather than the defeats. Then, like David, when the next crisis comes, I can encourage myself with, "The Lord who rescued my family from the ravages of sexual abuse will rescue us once again. I will put my hope in God! I will praise him again—my Savior and my God!"

Suggested Prayer Topics

Ask the Lord to show and remind you of the victories in your life. Write them down in a journal you can look back on when you are discouraged.

Lord, I Need a Friend

Gail Gritts

"I will never leave you, nor forsake you." Hebrews 13:5b NKJV

After over thirty years on the mission field, I have seen friends come and friends go. The reasons may vary, but they have moved in and out of my life at a steady pace. A few years ago, after being Stateside for over a year, I faced returning to the field with no close friends to welcome me back. My nearest friend was two hours away, and I was feeling the emptiness. So, that began my prayer, "Lord, please give me some friends." I had loads of folks around me in ministry, but I was missing the closeness that comes with two hearts bound in friendship outside the ministry context.

Once home, I continued my prayer and looked expectantly for my new friend. I tried developing friendships with those around me and reaching out where I believed was potential but came up dry. I continued my prayer and looked to the Lord as I waited for Him to bring me a real friend or two.

Then I got the dreadful news no one wants to hear. Cancer.

My concern for a friend waned as I began to draw upon my True Friend who faced the fears within me and helped me wade through decisions as a cancer patient. I needed help to understand what was happening and someone to guide me through the process. The only doctor I knew personally was the young wife of one of our former students, so I confided in her, and she became my confidant and source for decision making.

This young woman listened patiently as I explained my fears and queried every medicine and procedure. She took time to ask her colleagues and find the answers for me as she assured me of a good outcome. She met with me and sent little tokens of concern. She, too, lived over two hours away, but she took time to come and sit with me, and through this process, we became deep friends.

As Robert Browning put it, "Hush, I pray you! What if this friend happens to be—God?" Truly, God had answered my prayer. Her friendship was the hand of God in my life—His arms around me. Not only through my bout with cancer, but continuing today, her kindness and our unlikely friendship (as she puts it), is an answer to prayer.

Through counsel, comfort, sharing, and caring, friends are not only a gift from the Lord, they are tools in His hands. But friendship is a two-way street. God wants us to be a blessing to others, also.

My young friend faces a strenuous life. She is a wife and mother, a medical student, and a working doctor facing stresses most of us never know about the profession. In her times of need, God has allowed me to be her confidant and source of release and solace, causing our friendship to grow deeper as we do the give and take required to grow a friendship and keep it alive. Our unlikely friendship is a joy to us both.

We enjoy playing card games, walking on the beach, sipping cups of tea before the open fire, and old books. One she shared with me is *The Transforming Friendship* by Leslie D. Weatherhead. Written mainly about friendship with Christ, the author wrote, "When I go out to do a service to another man in the name of Christ, I feel I have not had an experience with that other man. I have had an experience with Christ."

And that must be the basis of a true friendship: to do good for someone else, to love them with an unselfish and generous spirit; to give to them as unto Christ. For only then will we be doing them a service. Only then will we recognize God amid our friendships.

As I look at my new friendship, I still see it as an answer to prayer. And God didn't stop by giving me one friend; I now have my young doctor friend, but also, two colleagues nearby for fun and encouragement; an older, solid friend who is like a mother; and beautiful, maturing friendships within ministry. With the arms of these friends around me, I see and feel the love of God—the everlasting arms—underneath, holding all of us up together. I'm never alone.

If you are feeling empty and lonely due to a lack of friends, call out to the True Friend and allow Him to bring people into your life to meet your need. They might be unlikely, but as He saw it was not good for Adam to be alone, He knows you need a companion as well. You never know who He will send your way, but you will feel His loving arms around you in the friendships He gives.

"Hush, I pray you! What if this friend happens to be—God?" (R. Browning).

Suggested Prayer Topics

Thank Jesus for your friends. Ask Him how you might be a better friend to the friends in your life. Ask Him to show you anyone who needs a friend and then reach out.

The Girl with the Saggy Socks

Dorothy Doswald

"Praying at all times in the Spirit, with all prayer and sup-
plication. To that end, keep alert with all perseverance,
making supplication for all the saints." Ephesians 6:18 ESV

Heavy clouds hid the early morning sky as we made our way to the car. The rain was predicted to begin at noon. Jenny and Mark strapped themselves in as I threw my purse and graded papers across the empty front seat.

After only a few miles an argument broke out behind me.

I looked in the rearview mirror. "What is going on, you two?"

"Mark's putting his feet on me! I told him not to, but he won't stop."

My son's face was the picture of innocence. I chose to change the subject instead of battle. "Do you see that little girl at the corner?" Both kids sat up tall. "Do you notice how her socks are puddled around her shoes? She seems so sad. Look at the way she is hanging her head."

"Why is she sad, Mommy?" my kindergarten son asked.

"I don't know. Do you have any ideas, Jenny?"

"I think her backpack is too heavy and her legs are cold." Jenny nodded.

"Maybe she's hungry," Mark suggested.

I noticed their concern. "What do you say we pray for this little girl to have a great day?" My kids nodded, and I led them in a simple prayer. The battle was averted.

Every morning, when we approached the corner, my kids would look for that little girl. Each day they had a different prayer request about her life. If I ever forgot to pray, they would loudly remind me. We prayed for her for three years until she mysteriously disappeared. The girl with the saggy socks was safely tucked away in our memories.

Fast forward seven years.

Our church's baptisms were to be held in our pool that summer day. I was busy putting treats on trays and making sure the lemonade jugs were full. People began to wander into our backyard. My kids, now teenagers, laughed with their friends and snatched cookies. A thin, beautiful young woman arrived with her mother. She looked vaguely familiar. "Hello. You must be here for the baptisms. Are either of you to be baptized today?"

"Yes, I'm going to be baptized. My name is Amanda*, and this is my mother, Susan*."

"How nice to meet you both." I pointed to the pastor who was talking to people near the pool. "Amanda, you are supposed to go over there for last minute instruction."

The young woman smiled before turning toward our pastor.

Looking at Amanda's mother, I caught a look of annoyance. "Susan, may I offer something to drink?"

Amanda's mother shook her head, "No, thank you."

"Your daughter is beautiful. I'm glad she has come to be a part of this service today," I said.

"Yes, she is beautiful and smart, too," Susan snapped.

"Well, I can tell. I can't wait to hear how she came to the Lord. Is your family from Clovis?"

"Yes, we live on the corner of Armstrong and Logan*."

I could feel my eyes grow wide as I touched her arm. "You live on the corner of Armstrong and Logan?"

Cocking her head, Susan paused before answering. "Yes, we do. Amanda's dad and I built the house twenty-five years ago. We raised all three of our kids there. Amanda is our youngest."

I looked across the yard and saw my pastor talking to Amanda. It couldn't be, could it? "Did your daughter wait for the school bus in front of your house?"

"Yes, she did."

"No way. It couldn't be." I shook my head incredulously.

Susan's brows pinched together. "Excuse me?"

"My two kids and I prayed for her every day for three years."

Susan crossed her arms and squinted her eyes. "Why? She is a good girl."

"The prayers began initially as a way to focus my kids on others. Then it grew into a sweet time with my kids learning to talk to God."

"What kinds of things did you pray for?"

"We prayed that she would have a good life, study hard, and have friends. We prayed for her to come to the Lord." I shrugged. "We prayed for anything. The prayers were simple but genuine."

"Amanda has had a good life. Although her father and I don't believe in God, my mother does. Her grandmother began taking her to church. I couldn't talk Amanda out of it. And here we are today," Susan moaned.

I smiled. "Well, I think it's a miracle. Something to teach me and my kids about how God answers prayer. It may have taken three years of praying and many years in between, but God is faithful."

I called both my children. When they were at my side, I introduced them to Susan and explained that she was the mother of the little girl with the saggy socks. Jenny's eyebrows rose as Mark's mouth dropped open. A slow smile spread across Jenny's face as she turned and sprinted across the grass and hugged Amanda.

God didn't have to bring Amanda to our own backyard. He chose to. The girl with the saggy socks taught me the power in a simple prayer. I call times like this a kiss from God.

And now we are praying for her parents.

Prayer is the way our life with God is nourished. God doesn't care about the length of our prayers or the eloquence of our words. He cares about our hearts. In our fast-paced world, prayer can sometimes be a quick sentence or two while in your car. Prayer isn't limited to the quiet of your home or church. When we pray for others, our eyes are lifted from our circumstances and centered on God. He loves us unconditionally and wants us to draw near to Him.

Suggested Prayer Topics

God desires that everyone comes to know Him. Are there people in your neighborhood, at work, or at school that you see every day but don't really know? Consider praying for them.

Names changed to protect privacy.

Ask God

DeeDee Lake

*"So we fasted and petitioned our God about this,
and he answered our prayer." Ezra 8:23 NIV*

A sk God for what you want."

My mentor's advice seemed a bit too simple when we were discussing another military move. This move was different. It was the first time we would relocate since my husband and I grew close to God.

"Ask God? Just ask Him like He is some sort of magic genie in the sky?" My tone revealed I didn't believe our Creator God cared about the details of my life. I may have rolled my eyes. "Seriously, I can ask God for anything?" I questioned her once again, still struggling to understand.

"Take some time and pray. Talk to Him. God is your heavenly Father and cares about what you care about."

I had spent nearly three years under Jane's mentoring and decided to give praying the way she suggested a chance. Months before we were to be transferred from Panama to Alabama, I began imagining and praying about my future house.

I dreamed my home would have rich wood floors, beautiful archways, a screened porch, lots and lots of big windows to fill each room with warm sunlight, a breakfast room, a large kitchen, a formal living room and a family room, a set of french doors, and a big safe, fenced-in backyard. Every time I began to fret over the details, I would stop and pray.

I knew I'd given God a big list. I also knew our God is a big God and able to do all things. In the meantime, I waited on the Lord and trusted Him to work it all out.

The time came for my husband and me to take a short trip up to Alabama for house hunting before the big move. These were the days before the internet, and we needed to put boots on the ground to be able to see the homes for sale in the Fort Rucker area. My husband wanted to drive down Broad Street. The wide street in the old section of town lined with antebellum homes was like a glimpse into a bygone era.

"Seth, we won't be able to afford any house on this street. This is where the mayor, doctors, and lawyers live. You know it's out of our price range." I was sure God did not have a house for us on this tree-lined road.

Seth wasn't dissuaded. "Let's just go check it out." The sweet smile he gave me convinced me to trust him. I thought, if nothing else, it is a beautiful drive. We passed enormous homes filled with Southern charm and when we were nearly at the end of the road, he spotted a quaint home for sale. He whipped the rental car around and pulled into the driveway. The home was empty, and the yard a bit overgrown.

"Let's go peek in the windows." Seth's excitement was contagious.

I agreed to take a quick look. The three gable windows across the front of the house caught my attention. Then I saw the wonderful set of french front doors. I had never been in a house with french doors for the front door. I couldn't believe this was the exact house I prayed about in Panama.

We walked around the house and quickly realized it was deceiving from the road. It was quaint but very large. We walked into the adorable screened porch of my prayers. The door creaked a bit as we continued our trespassing. Standing side-by-side with our faces pressed into one of the many large windows, we heard someone speak from behind us. We turned around and I greeted the man with the Southern graces I was raised with.

The man was the owner who came to check on the property. God brought the owner at the very same time we were falling in love with this french cottage built in the early 1920s. The gracious man opened the doors for us to explore.

Rich hardwood floors stretched from room to room. The three formal rooms, each with arched, glass french doors between them, also had a large gas fireplace in the center room. The formal rooms' arched ceilings were twelve feet high to match the arched doorways. Floor-to-ceiling built in bookshelves lined the hallway to the sunroom at the back of the house. It was delightful, with windows all around and a huge tiger-oak wood fireplace.

I struggled not to giggle with joy. I needed to put on my game face so the seller wouldn't up his price.

When the kind older gentlemen realized we were a military family, he said he wanted to bless us. He priced the house under market value. Our little french cottage was even lower than the budget God impressed upon us as we prayed through each stage of the purchase.

Everything I talked to my heavenly Father about was there and so much more. I asked for one set of french doors. He delivered three. I counted thirty-nine amazing windows. The morning sun poured through them as we walked from room to room. I imagined cooking in the kitchen with its high ceilings. The backyard was a fenced-in sanctuary. Along the back of the property were sweet smelling leafy bushes.

God heard my heart and answered every detail of my prayers.

Suggested Prayer Topics

God loves to bless His children and answer their prayers. He cares about the details of your life. Today, go before the Lord with your specific cares and needs. Pray, expect, and watch for God's answers.

Graduation Gift

Debbie Jones Warren

"Though he brings grief, he will show compassion, so great is his unfailing love." Lamentations 3:32 NIV

*W*ould you pray that my parents can come to my graduation?" I asked the young women in my college Bible study. "My mom and dad are missionaries in Nigeria, and they have a whole year to go before their next furlough, but we graduate in four months."

While the other girls would have their parents in the audience, applauding this big step in life, mine didn't have time off. Even if the mission board granted them leave, they had no money for airfare.

I longed for Mom and Dad to share this major milestone with me, so I dared ask for the impossible. In January, I wrote a letter. My parents had no telephone or internet, and my note took four to five weeks to reach inland Africa. Their reply traveled back by ocean freighter, forcing me to wait yet another month.

With trembling fingers, I slit open the top of the envelope and pulled out the lined, white stationery bearing my mom's familiar handwriting. Nothing would make us happier than to be there with you when you graduate. But we just can't leave right now.

My lower lip trembled as tears blurred the words. In my heart, I heard a heavy iron gate clang shut on my dream.

As a child, I had lived in southwestern Nigeria with my missionary family. Our cozy village station lay nestled in a semi-circle of hills studded with rocky outcroppings and savannah brush. But beginning in first grade, I attended boarding school 300 miles away, only returning home for Christmas and summer vacations.

During those lengthy separations from family, I suffered from intense homesickness. Many nights I cried alone in bed, feeling abandoned by God and my parents. By fourth grade I "toughened up" and accepted that way of life as normal, but the wounds remained.

When I began college in California, my parents continued their work in Nigeria, and the transition to a college dorm proved difficult. I felt constant confusion while trying to assimilate into this new culture.

To numb the ache, I immersed myself in my classes and my job. But I couldn't ignore the simmering anger. I resented my parents for putting their ministry ahead of me, and I blamed God for my loneliness.

Then I chided myself for wanting my family to live closer. A lot of kids have moved from home to attend universities in other states. I'm so weak and immature. Do I really need Mommy and Daddy at this age? I never had them before.

In my final semester, when I shared my wish with my Bible study friends, my tongue tripped over the words. It seemed like such a petty request.

"God cares about all our concerns," my friend Beth said. "He loves to give good gifts." The girls added me to their prayers.

However, two huge, unspoken questions droned over and over in my mind like helicopters circling above a crime scene: Is God able to break through these impossible barriers? And if He can, does He care enough?

In mid-May, the phone in my apartment kitchen rang. When I heard my father's voice, I sank into a kitchen chair. Something must be terribly wrong for him to call long distance.

"Dad? Where are you?" Alarming scenarios whirled through my mind.

"I just landed at San Francisco airport," he began with his distinct low drawl. "I need medical treatment for a problem with my prostate."

"Oh, no." The words squeaked out while my heart pounded to the beat of an African drum.

He continued with a soft chuckle, adding his trademark humor. "On the bright side, Mom's here with me. We'll both be in the stands, whooping and hollering, when you collect your diploma next weekend."

"I can't wait to see you. I've missed you so much." Dropping the phone into the cradle, I screamed, "I don't believe it!"

"What on earth happened?" My roommate poked her head out her bedroom doorway.

"My parents just flew in." The prickle at the back of my nose signaled I needed a tissue. "While I was praying, God was preparing their way."

As I hugged my roommate, I silently wondered, how is it possible that God answered my prayer through something as crazy as Dad needing treatment for his prostate?

On the big day, several hundred graduates promenaded through the rows of metal folding chairs on the university football field. Dad and Mom grabbed seats in the closest row, and I heard their voices cheering above everyone else's.

The next week, Dad had his operation for prostate cancer. While we waited for him to come out of surgery, Mom described the extraordinary circumstances that brought them to California, beginning with Dad's crisis of pain while driving to a remote Nigerian village.

"Through God's perfect timing, we were just an hour from the only hospital in that rural region," Mom said.

Soon the surgeon pushed open the waiting room door, and his voice boomed out reassurance. "We got all the cancer."

After several weeks of rest, Dad and Mom flew back to their teaching ministry in Nigeria, and I started my first full-time job, brimming with confidence that stemmed from my new-found conviction of God's unfailing love.

In His sovereignty, God sometimes allows loss, loneliness, and grief to touch our lives as it says in Lamentations 3:32. But He also brings healing, redemption, and reconciliation. His Father-heart is always filled with deep love for us, even though we may not feel it during tough times.

Has there been a point in your life when you felt lost, alone, and abandoned by God or others? How did you cope? What are some ways you've seen God providing for you or proving His love to you?

Suggested Prayer Topics

Pray for children of missionaries, medical staff, military personnel, and government workers who live around the world.

Pathway to Paradise

Catherine Ulrich Brakefield

"Rejoicing in hope, patient in tribulation, continuing steadfastly in prayer." Romans 12:12 NKJV

My dad was the Rock of Gibraltar of our family. My son and daughter admired and looked up to him as did my husband and I. So, when Dad was diagnosed with Parkinson's disease, we couldn't comprehend what that would mean to our family!

The most difficult time was somewhere between my mom's death and learning the truth about Dad. My faith was shaken right down to its foundation.

It was easy for me to pray for others who were going through tribulation. Easy to pray and believe Proverbs 3:5,6: "Trust in the LORD with all your heart, And lean not on your own understanding; In all your ways acknowledge Him, And He shall direct your paths" (NKJV).

Confronted with decisions that would affect Dad's lifestyle, I wasn't so confident. How did I know if I was following God's will or my own selfish desires? I asked God for a sign.

I felt like I was standing on a seesaw. Would God's unconditional love penetrate my doubt? Would my love for God prove strong enough to bear the burden of decision-making and tending my dad until God took him home? When Mom died on January 6, 2006, Dad acted lost. With the help of a caregiver, Dad had taken care of her throughout the years of her debilitating stroke and cancer. I had hoped Dad would return to Michigan so I could care for my mom as I had her mother for twelve years. Dad decided to remain in Florida with Mom and hired a caregiver to help him.

After Mom's funeral, I attributed his stumbling, choking on food, his hands shaking uncontrollably, to the loss of his true love. When the symptoms continued, I asked, "Dad, what's wrong." He confessed he had Parkinson's.

The caregiver who helped with my mom, now took care of my dad. We soon learned we couldn't live in Michigan and leave Dad in Florida and trust his safety to a caregiver.

I discovered this when Dad came for a visit at Christmas. He told me one day to bring in his great-grandson who was sitting outside on a snowdrift during an afternoon snowstorm. I gently told Dad he was seeing things. He looked at me and nodded. "Cath, I figured so. You wouldn't let him do that."

The next morning, he reached for his glass of orange juice but picked up an imaginary glass. He brought it to his lips and drank, then he set the imaginary glass down and said, "Well, that didn't taste like much." I rushed forward, picked up the glass of orange juice sitting in front of him and said, "Here, try this."

Part of Parkinson's symptoms is hallucinations, but to this degree? Dad needed my help big time. No way was Dad going to move to Michigan. He was used to holding the reins, and we were used to asking him what to do, not vice versa.

"Please, Jesus," I prayed, "help me. What should I do?" Then, needing something from the drug store, I scooped up Dad's pill boxes and drove to the pharmacy. I asked the pharmacist to check the pills against the prescriptions.

The caregiver had incorrectly dispensed Dad's medications, and he was getting triple the dose of Mirapex! With this corrected, his hallucinations stopped.

I explained it all to Dad. He took a step back and flopped down on his bed, a look of complete disbelief written across his face.

The next day, Dad was dozing in the recliner. He woke up and said to me, "Cath, I miss your mom. I'll never marry again. But I don't want to go the way she did, in a hospital bed. I want to go standing on my own two feet."

Only God could answer that prayer. I hoped He was listening!

I had promised Dad he would not be placed in a senior care center or nursing home. But after what I saw with the current caregiving staff, I couldn't trust them. My siblings and I had to do the only thing left to do.

We fired that caregiver and hired another. In fact, we hired quite a few. It became evident Dad needed one of us around. But we had our jobs and our own families to care for.

"God," I pleaded, "'[Love] bears all things, believes all things, hopes all things, endures all things. Love never fails.' (1 Corinthians 13:7,8). Where is Your love? Lord, help me. Where are You when I need You?"

The years began to take their toll on us. Dad would stay with us in Michigan during the summer, then my siblings and I would rotate spending two to three weeks in Florida during the winter. Dad didn't notice his deteriorating health. He wanted to date, and in Florida there were plenty of women who would date a man old enough to be their father.

Then came another disheartening report. The doctor warned

us Dad's dementia was worsening, that he may forget who we are!

I felt my prayers hitting a brick wall. Dad was growing hostile toward me. His women friends made him feel young, and he saw no reason why he couldn't date them. Why wasn't God helping us?

More doctor visits. We prayed we were doing the right thing. Should we hire more help? "Lord, please give me a sign, some sign, that what we are doing with Dad is what You want us to do." Romans 12:12 came to mind: "Rejoicing in hope, patient in tribulation, continuing steadfastly in prayer."

It was January 6, 2012, my sister's turn to be with Dad. About six months earlier, one of Dad's doctors told him he had the heart of a twenty-year-old. At least we could rule out heart attack. My sister had just brought Dad back from seeing one of his specialist doctors.

Dad was watching television. My sister, her husband, and Dad's nurse were sitting alongside him. Suddenly, Dad stood and told my sister he was going home. My sister, thinking it was dementia, said, "Dad, you are home."

Dad smiled. "Yeah, well, I'll see ya later."

He took a step forward and dropped to the floor. The nurse rushed to his side, seeking a pulse. "He's gone."

That day God demonstrated His unconditional love for me by performing a sign I could not ignore. When I thought God wasn't listening, when I thought it was I who had to bear all things, His unconditional love bore the burden unequivocally. Proverbs 3:5,6 held true. "In all thy ways acknowledge Him, and He shall direct thy paths."

God planned His own happy ending to our prayers!

My siblings and I reminisce in amazement how God gave us His sign we were doing His will—that special gift only a loving Jesus could give—when Dad started his walk toward his heavenly home on January 6, the same date Mom died six years before.

Suggested Prayer Topics

*P*ray wisdom, strength, and guidance for those caring for family members and those they are caring for.

Out of the Corner

Molly Woods

*"The gatekeeper opens the gate for him, and the
sheep listen to his voice. He calls his own sheep by
name and leads them out." John 10:3 NIV*

Whispers. I've heard them my whole life.

No, I'm not crazy. I don't mean actual whispers. I'm talking about God whispers, those little nudges of spirit. And then, at one critical point, that whispering became a full-throated shout. It's humbling to talk about. My life was a mess when God made me a priority and used His God voice. It wasn't when I was living well or according to His word. On the contrary, I was in the dark. The full dark. Nothing in me felt deserving of such divine attention. We all have stories. In a way, part of my story makes me think of Christmas morning. It makes me feel like a child standing open-mouthed, staring at that perfect gift under the tree and breathlessly asking, "Really, that's for me?"

God came to me in just that way. During the grittiest of circumstances, He made me feel cherished. Special. Loved. So loved. He came to me during the chaos of my addiction. I was at the end of that road, sitting on my bed, ready to take my own life.

The full details aren't important, but a few are necessary. I had been married for twenty years, had two children, and my divorce was nearly finalized. I'm a nurse and I was working in a local emergency room. I was good at my job and my pride had grown into an oily arrogance, cleverly disguised by false humility. I was respected, liked, and trusted with friends and a future. And I was lost. "Naked in the dark" kind of lost. I couldn't keep the masks on. They were slipping. In active addiction, the only thing in control is the addiction. I've never felt so alone while surrounded by people.

Things had taken a turn. I was suspended from work and waiting to see if I had a job, a career, a future. I was alone. Desperate. Terrified out of my mind. I sat on my bed with my gun loaded, certain there was no way out. It was like sitting in a frigid dark corner, trapped and strangled by a hopelessness so dense the only solution I could see was taking my own life. It still hurts my gut to even remember it.

I picked up my gun. And God shouted. With my phone sitting silent on the bed, as clear as a real picture in front of me, I saw my cell phone screen with my daughter's name illuminated as if she was calling. Like lightning, my mind fired through several things at once. If I killed myself, who would answer when my daughter called? Her mom wouldn't be able to. What would this do to my son? My mom? Anyone who loved me? It snapped me out of myself and that cold dark corner at exactly the right last moment. In the middle of my depravity, God chose to step in with me. And shout at me. And save me.

I emptied the gun and called my mom. I got real. I got honest. I asked for help. And because my mom is as true as they come, she dropped everything and came to stay with me. She helped me walk through the wreckage. My mom loves our Lord, and He used her to love me through the hell I'd helped create.

That shout was only the beginning. God kept at me, providing a way through that shouldn't have been a way through. He removed obstacles to my future in such a way that the word miracle is too small. I have no other explanation for how I kept my nursing license or was able to accept the reality of being a recovering addict. As prideful and lost as I was, He kept at it with His relentless outpouring of one graceful provision after another. It was so blatant and bold, even in my self-obsessed spin, I could see His hand…in everything.

And slowly, so subtly I didn't realize it was happening, I started to feel…safe. Loved. Important. Worthy. And like only God can do, something started to awaken. Hope. The real kind. There's no fairy dust on real hope. The hope that started then was born in the muck and mire, resilient and made of steel. Of course it was. It was rooted in pure love. His love.

That hope has yielded such richness. Today I'm an entirely different human. I'm thriving. With nearly six years clean, my life looks nothing like it did on that dark-corner day. Has it taken work? You bet. And while I dug my heels in and got in God's way at first, His steady love always nudged me just a little farther. Forward. Whenever I came up against myself as I worked my recovery program and felt stuck, there was always this persistent tap on my shoulder. Like a whisper to my spirit with a relentless gentleness that said: "Oh my warrior princess, remember who you are. You are beloved. And you got this." And so, I would step again. Forward. At times petulant as a child, but always forward.

Those steps have brought me…here. I'm going to keep walking with my beautiful Savior. I don't need to see the whole road anymore before I take a step. I know who's leading me, and God only takes me to the best places. Now I'm curious and excited to see what He has in mind.

I'll keep walking. Until I'm home.

As we go about the business of working with God to become the best version of ourselves, our minds can "get in the way." We all have old patterns of thinking that affect our behavior. The one true power we all possess is our power to choose whom we listen to. As you go about your day, choose to redirect your thoughts the way God suggests in John 10:3: "The gatekeeper opens the gate for him, and the sheep listen to his voice. He calls his own sheep by name and leads them out." Transformation is a lifelong process of one deliberate response after another. Allow God's Word to help you choose well.

Suggested Prayer Topics

Ask Jesus to make His voice clearly discernible in your life and the lives of those around you.

Walking Through Darkness with the Light of the World

Cheryl J. Heser

"Answer me when I call to you, O God who declares me innocent. Free me from my troubles." Psalm 4:1 NLT

The final chapter of my son Josh's life began in an unpredictable accident on a country road. A low tire on the open Bronco came too close to the edge of a ravine and tumbled the vehicle down while four people were catapulted out. Three of them staggered to their feet and discovered Josh lying inert where his head had hit a large rock. The driver performed CPR while the others begged through cell phones for help, and Josh breathed quietly as an ambulance screamed, a helicopter whisked through black skies, and the emergency staff of Benefis East Hospital whirled into action.

That night we received the call no parents ever want to experience and drove 300 agonizing miles to Great Falls, Montana, arriving just a few hours before our beloved son, only thirty-three years old, was pronounced brain dead. Our older son and daughter and families arrived, and we clung to each other through that unbelievable day. I sobbed and tried to read since I could not sleep that night. At about 4:30 in the morning, when I finally was dozing, I was awakened by my perpetually early-rising husband and beckoned to a hall window, where he had discovered the sign that would sustain him through the months to come. In the morning sky, shone a star with a perfect cross over it.

In a moment's thought I return there. Breathless, we behold the brilliance of the cross manifested in starlight. Like the Christmas star beckoning to shepherds and kings to welcome the Christ, this star welcomes our beloved son into eternity. Interstellar travel bursts on the wings of eagles at the speed of light—and his death and our lives become transformed. Easter's wooden cross, changed from dross to gold, shines as brightly as the Christmas star, fulfilling the promise, turning the wise men's rich gifts into the richer gift of salvation.

As my thoughts indicate, we are people of strong Christian faith. Without doubt, we knew from the morning of the star that our son Joshua was in heaven, safe in the outstretched arms of God, and that we would see him again when we, too, were there in heaven. However, belief was a tiny boat cresting over wave after wave in a turbulent sea of desperate memories and barreling into troughs of despair. I could not perform as captain, navigator, or even assistant but could only cling to the side and watch Josh's life pass before my eyes.

If the story of Josh ended with my grief, I would not have shared this experience. Instead I must take you back to the moment of Josh's brain death. With his head covered with a white cloth, Josh was lying hooked to a respirator that kept his lungs working and heart beating, sustaining his body warm and "alive" as a team prepared for harvesting organs and body parts that would eventually change the lives of over 100 people.

During those days of waiting, much of my time was spent holding his huge hand, which was unresponsive but warm and touchable. Miraculously, I felt his strength flowing into me like a healing river, sustaining me, enabling me to deal with his death. To this day I feel that strength.

Second, as Josh lay there, his left lung, slightly damaged when he was thrown from the vehicle, actually miraculously healed to the point that it could be used for a transplant. Can you imagine the body healing in such a way even after the brain no longer functions?! Praise God for the amazing bodies He has created for us! The recipient of Josh's lungs is now living a full life, engaged to be married, and, coincidentally, just retired from running his own mechanics business like Josh's.

Those miracles and my eventual emergence from personal darkness are all because of God's will made present in our lives through Jesus. I have come to the point of knowing Jesus is present to help bear our burdens and to guide us to the point where we see that God works through all things, no matter how tragic, for blessings in our lives.

Everyone deals with times of grief, deep sadness, or depression at different levels, and many families deal with the death of a child or sibling. If we seek the light of Jesus and make every day a time of walking with Him and reading and following His words, we will find His light penetrating our darkness and giving us strength and resilience to continue our lives in a positive way.

You see, the difference between walking in darkness and walking with Jesus is the preposition. With gives us a companion on the journey. Those suffering from grief or depression—

from any condition that leaves them in the darkness—learn that it is a solitary, lonely journey. Groping in the darkness saps the spirit, tires the body, and addles the mind. Help lies in reaching out and grasping the hand Jesus offers. Then the Light dawns. In addition, we find the journey is no longer solitary because others are grasping His hand as well. We can reach for the people who personify the Light—those people all around us whom the Light shines through.

My awareness of the worth and fragility of life, the need for living with respect for every day and every person in it, and the value of conscious love of those around us has increased exponentially. I pray more often, I treasure God's love more deeply, and I thank God in all things. Do these gifts come from me? No, they come from God made flesh, Jesus who lives within me and walks beside me.

Suggested Prayer Topics

Ask Jesus to keep you close beside Him every day and to keep you aware of how precious you are to Him, as well as every person you care about.

Delivered

Debra L. Butterfield

"I sought the LORD, and He heard me, And delivered me from all my fears." Psalm 34:4 NKJV

W ho wants to admit they have a phobia? Certainly I didn't want to. After all, fear comes from the devil (2 Timothy 1:7). But in truth, a phobia had control of my life.

My daughter was to graduate in December with her master's degree. I needed a vacation from my busy work schedule. So, I decided to treat my daughter and grandson to a trip to Orlando, Florida. It would be a wonderful graduation present for her, an extra special Christmas present for my grandson, and a vacation for me. I would drive to Arkansas for the graduation and the following day, we would start the drive to Orlando.

But I faced every trip with trepidation due to a digestive issue that went undiagnosed for over a decade. Would there be a bathroom when I needed it? Doctors had diagnosed me with irritable bowel, so I attributed the digestive issue to IBS. I later determined the issue as lactose intolerance, but by then I had developed an unconscious reaction to any kind travel. Just the thought of travel could set me off, but I refused to let fear stop me. I resorted to over-the-counter medicines, which helped, but I couldn't enjoy any trip.

As two days on the road to Florida stared me in the face, fear roared at me. I countered it by quoting God's promises of healing and claiming other biblical promises. It helped, but it was an every day moment-by-moment battle.

The day arrived to leave for Arkansas. I taught English at our church's private school from eight o'clock to nine, and after class I'd hit the road. I'd come close to canceling the trip to Florida because of the physical turmoil I was already experiencing. The lactose intolerance had resolved itself when I stopped using milk, but my body seemed to have a mind of its own. I knew how disappointed my daughter and grandson would be if I canceled, and I didn't want to give that kind of power to this fear.

After class I sought my pastor and asked him to pray. He had the school principal join us. She is a mighty prayer warrior in our church. Together we began to pray. The moment Pastor identified the issue as a phobia, my spirit agreed. My head didn't want to, but even in my reason I recognized this had become a phobia.

As Matthew 18:18 commands us to bind the enemy, we bound that fear. We claimed 1 Peter 2:24, that by Jesus' stripes I was healed. When their prayer was over, I knew I had been healed and delivered. I rejoiced in the Lord the whole six-hour drive to Arkansas.

A few days later as we packed my daughter's car and headed to Florida, instead of fear, excitement about the trip filled my spirit. My daughter knew of my issue and occasionally asked me how I was doing. I answered "great."

At one point, ten hours into the first day on the road (we

traveled thirteen before we stopped for the night), that fear attempted an ambush. I quoted Psalm 34:4, 1 Peter 2:24, Psalm 23, and more to myself to combat it. It fled.

This fear had assaulted me for over twenty years, having grown worse each year to the point of phobia. Hallelujah, God delivered me!

Oh yes, fear still rears its ugly head. Not just fear of traveling, but in other ways. I quote Psalm 34:4 and rest in the fact the God "delivered me from *all* my fears" (emphasis mine).

Suggested Prayer Topics

*P*ray for the Lord to bind the spirit of fear that attacks people around the world every day. Pray for the Holy Spirit to help us depend on God for our all needs and give Him all our worries and fears.

Dear Abba Father

Carol Round

"And I will be your Father, and you will be my sons and daughters, says the Lord Almighty." 2 Corinthians 6:18 NLT

Linda, I'm forty-seven years old, but I don't know who I am," I told my friend as we power walked around the oval track.

"What do you mean?" she asked.

"Well, I'm my parents' daughter, an empty nest mother, and a high school teacher," I replied. "But, I'm no longer anyone's wife."

Before she could reply, I answered my own question, surprised at my sudden aha moment. "Wait, I know who I am. I'm a daughter of the highest God."

"And that's the most important identity of all." She smiled.

My twenty-eight-year marriage had ended amicably several months before. We'd attended counseling sessions, together and independently. Early in our sessions, the counselor suggested I begin keeping a prayer or spiritual journal.

In the beginning, my written pleas in the form of a letter were addressed to "Dear God." Many of my entries had been,

"Please change my husband's heart."

Every seven years, my husband had asked for a divorce. He'd decided we had nothing in common, except our sons. Not wanting our children to be raised in a broken home, I worked hard to please him.

After our youngest left for college, I questioned my commitment to the marital relationship. Was I ready for the next seven-year cycle? Could I face the fear of abandonment and the turmoil that would follow? What if my husband asked for a divorce? Would I give in or just give up?

I continued to write in my journal each day. Still, I never felt peace, the peace that passes understanding. Returning to counseling after a five-year hiatus, I updated her on my feelings and what was going on in my marriage. She reminded me I'd never really been on my own. I'd gone from living with my parents to a college dorm for two years and then becoming a wife at nineteen.

"I suggest a separation before you consider a divorce," she said.

It wasn't easy to leave. I'd always felt like I was my husband's keeper, his mother, who had to remind him of birthdays and other important events; get him up on time for work or else he'd sleep through the alarm; and make appointments for his doctor, dental, and other visits. While I did those things out of love, I'd begun to resent his dependency, the threat of abandonment, the suspicion of infidelity.

As our month-long separation came to an end, I realized a truth. My husband didn't love me as I had hoped to love and be loved. More importantly, I knew I was not the person God had created me to be.

The Bible says God frowns on divorce but staying in an emotionally controlling marriage was not the path forward for me, my husband, or my family.

I confess that although I had grown up attending church, I'd drifted away time and again, especially after I married. Following the divorce, my spiritual journal became a lifeline, a beginning of something I'd never experienced before, an intimate loving relationship with God through His Son, Jesus Christ.

About two months after our divorce was final, I was struggling to finish a magazine article for a Christian publication. I'd never encountered writer's block, but I'd hit a wall and my deadline was looming.

Stepping away from my computer, I laced up my running shoes and headed outdoors for some fresh air—and hopefully, some inspiration. Walking toward the nearby lake, I was compelled to do something I'd never done before. At the edge of our neighborhood is a picnic area, complete with picnic tables. I'd never ventured to sit down at one and just enjoy the lake teeming with geese and pelicans. I'd always been in hurry-up mode, running or walking fast to burn calories and deal with stress.

But that day, I was led by the Holy Spirit to stop, sit, and pray aloud for the very first time. My simple prayer that day was, "God, I need some direction in my life. Please help me."

Peace flooded my spirit. It felt as if a backpack of rocks had been lifted from my back. Returning home after finishing my walk, I was able to complete the story and meet my deadline.

My relationship with God began to grow as evidenced in my daily journaling. Instead of writing "Dear God" when I began an entry, my pen immediately flowed with the words, "Dear Abba Father."

Since that day, my Abba Father has empowered me to put aside the need to perform, to be a people pleaser to earn the love of others. God has helped me overcome the past, to forgive. Today, my former husband and I have established a friendly relationship based on what we have in common, what we both love, our two sons and seven grandchildren.

Suggested Prayer Topics

If you've never tried writing out your prayers in the form of a love letter to your Abba Father, why not grab a spiral notebook or buy a pretty journal and commit to forty days of journaling your thoughts and your thanks to the One who loves you more than life itself. As you continue to pen your words to Him, notice how much closer you begin to draw to your Creator— Your Abba Father.

God's Hidden Surprise

Donna Wyland

"May he [God] *give you the desire of your heart…May he remember all your sacrifices." Psalm 20:4a, 3a NIV*

A m I doing the right thing, Lord?" I asked as I slipped the one carat engagement ring from my finger. Tucking it between tissue paper in a cheap white box, I closed the lid and sighed. Then I slid onto the driver's seat, heart racing with fear. I had texted my soon to be ex-fiancé and told him I'd meet him at his townhouse after work.

"If I am hearing you wrong, Lord, stop me now. Please don't make me do this. Don't leave me alone for the rest of my life."

Throughout the drive—the longest one of my life—God and I had a running conversation. I have to admit I was doing most—okay, maybe all—of the talking, pleading for confirmation of what I thought the Holy Spirit was leading me to do.

But why? Why would God want to hurt us so much? Why would He want us apart when we seemed to be such a good fit?

When I pulled up behind my fiancé's car, I wanted to snatch

the ring out of the box and slide it right back on my finger. I wanted to feel secure again, like I belonged to someone who loved me, someone who would promise to never leave me alone.

The moment he opened the front door, he seemed to know what I was about to say. He glanced at my bare ring finger. "Are you breaking up with me?"

I wanted so much to say, "No. I love you. I want to spend the rest of my life with you." But instead, God led me to say, "I can't explain why, but my spirit is disturbed. I believe God is telling me I cannot marry you."

I laid the small box on his dining room table and quickly turned to leave, but he followed me out the door, pressing for an explanation. Sadly, I couldn't give him one. It felt wrong to hurt him so much. To hurt myself. What had I done?

Weeping the whole way home, I begged God to restore what I had just broken. Then I spent the rest of the day binge-watching Hallmark movies, bursting into tears every time things worked out and the couple ended up together. Oh, how I wanted our story to end the same way.

The truth is, while my fiancé and I regularly attended church the two and a half years we dated, my fiancé's faith pretty much stopped there. He had recently been baptized, but God knew we were unequally yoked. And deep down, so did I.

While we dated, I had prayed that my fiancé would supernaturally connect with God, that the "light bulb" would go off, and he would begin the adventure of walking close to Jesus. But now I see I wasn't fooling God for one second. He saw how I had compromised my love for Him and elevated my fiancé to first place in my life.

I still began each day with devotions, Bible reading, and prayer as I had for more than twenty years, but my heart was moving away from God. I recognized I couldn't hear His voice as well as I once did, but I didn't want to admit it was because of me.

In the two weeks following our broken engagement, my fiancé and I did not communicate. Then, with encouragement from my pastor, I texted my fiancé and arranged a meeting. Before he arrived, I prayed the Holy Spirit would be in our words and in our hearts.

To my amazement, the moment he walked through my front door, my fiancé began to tell me how God had opened his heart and spoken to him. He listed the ways God showed him he had let me down. Then he went on to tell of his newfound passion for Bible reading, his new membership in a men's small group, and his recent commitment to a weekly Bible study.

I was stunned. I had prayed for him to love Jesus throughout our entire relationship, and there he was telling me how the Holy Spirit had spoken to his heart. I wanted to jump into his arms as he expressed his love for God and his excitement about a relationship with Jesus.

But I felt the Holy Spirit cautioning me to wait upon the Lord, to watch and see if my fiancé's newfound faith would grow or fall away as we each sought God independently for a time before reconsidering a dating relationship.

Throughout the next seven months, we met at church on Sunday mornings, joined a couple's Bible study, and slowly began to date again with godly friends praying for us and speaking encouragement to us. The next time my fiance proposed, my answer was a confident yes.

As we grow closer to God together, I understand more clearly why He led us to wait. My fiance wasn't the only one God wanted to transform and draw closer to Him. I needed some work, too.

I'm so grateful for God's protection that kept us from marrying too soon. Grateful for His intervention in my fiancé's life. Even grateful for the sacrifices He was asking us to make along the way.

Learning to trust the still small voice of God and follow the movement of the Holy Spirit is a learning experience through which God is teaching me to be secure in His love, confident that He will never leave me alone. It is God's love, not man's, that I've been craving my whole life.

And because God knows my deep desire for a godly life partner, I can trust His desire to fulfill it in His time.

God is the same yesterday, today, and forever (Hebrews 13:8). And part of His unchanging nature is His promise of blessing for obedience, even if it means making difficult decisions that temporarily break our hearts. Doing life God's way guarantees the best possible outcome. Develop a deep connection with God, listen for His voice through the Holy Spirit, and courageously do what He asks, confident that His desire is to grant you the desire of your heart.

Suggested Prayer Topics

Pray for an open heart to receive and for courage to act when the Holy Spirit whispers the will of God to you.

He Drew Us All

Nancy Enna Cowart

"The Lord has appeared of old to me, saying: 'Yes, I have loved you with an everlasting love; Therefore with lovingkindness I have drawn you.'" Jeremiah 31:3 NKJV

My parents did a fine day's work. They loved me well. When I married my husband, he and his parents continued with what my own parents had begun.

Though my husband's mother never went to college, she had great zeal for education. Before my daughters began preschool, she taught them to memorize nursery rhymes, write their names, and draw pictures of people, places, and things. She loved them well.

When my daughters were still tender in age, I worked as a beauty consultant. Even though my husband's mother expressed interest in me "fixing up her eyes," I never did. I feared her sensitive skin might not fare well with the products I sold.

She always used the same moisturizing cream. It suited her skin. As to makeup, she seldom wore anything beyond eyebrow pencil. Even powder and lipstick were reserved for special occasions. My husband's mother never mentioned anything about eye makeup again and my beauty consultant days were short lived. Yet, I kept a quiet regret over not having had that experience with her.

The grandchildren grew up and the grandparents grew old. When my husband's mother took sick—a sickness unto death—our family rallied together to help her move into eternity. She died peacefully in her own bed slathered down in her own trusty moisturizing cream.

My husband and I moved through our grief. As empty nesters, we savored our quiet time together. Our daughters had their own lives but lived in the same town. During this time, our youngest began to struggle with anxiety. With our support she sought professional help but never said much about it otherwise. And she graduated college with honors and began a job search.

As my lunch hour approached one Friday, my youngest phoned in tears over a problem at her job. We met in the parking lot of my workplace. I drove and listened while she relayed the unexpected scene of the day. We departed sometime later in the same parking lot, but not before I learned that she and her roommate were a couple. The roommate—a mother of two very young children—had visited in our home and had begun attending the same church where we worship.

I further learned that my daughter's therapist had been advising her to find the courage to tell me about the relationship.

While I was completely unprepared for such a revelation, we parted peacefully, and I returned to work. After managing through the remainder of the day, I took the news home to my husband. I found him no wiser of the relationship than what I had been.

The week thereafter is now a memory. A painful memory.

The most painful of our lives. Too broken to leave our home, all I could manage were prayers, tears, and sleep. I took the following verse to bed with me, holding it like a pillow:

"The LORD is close to the brokenhearted and saves those who are crushed in spirit" (Psalm 34:18 NIV).

It's amazing what a person dreams in the state of a crushed spirit. Yet, dream I did. I was a young mother once again with my youngest fretting in a manner so alien to the baby we knew. Our baby carried a perfectly pitched tune before she learned to talk. But the baby before me wouldn't sing. She refused to be comforted.

With her situated around my hip, I suddenly looked up to find my husband's mother.

"Help me—what do I do?" I pleaded.

My husband's mother said nothing. She simply dismissed the matter with a wave of her hand. A wave so unique to her. And then, in a fleeting moment—like a flash—I saw her face.

Lovely eyes enhanced with makeup. And then, she was gone.

I awoke to the fragrance of moisturizing cream—again, something so unique to my husband's mother. That comforting smell had been discussed countless times by our family. But nary a word, at any time, had ever been uttered about my never having fixed up her eyes with makeup.

The dream stayed with me. A few years have now passed and it's with me still.

Only the Lord, who appeared of old, declaring His everlasting love to His people, could orchestrate such a scene of comfort. In that dream, He allowed me to see that, while no one else knew my regret about my husband's mother, He knew. And since He knew that about me, then He also knew the state of my crushed spirit. He also knew the source of my daughter's anxiety. An anxiety that, though unknown, even alien to me, felt very real to her.

I believe God, my heavenly Father, saw me taking that Scripture to bed with me. Out of love and kindness, He responded. He drew me close—closer than my pillow. He sent a dream and a comforting fragrance to remind me that He knows me and is always with me. That dream helped me realize that regret, anxiety, and a crushed spirit are things only God can fix. Only He can comfort and soothe. Only He can heal and restore.

Long before I felt crushed in spirit, God, my heavenly Father, drew me in yet another way. Not unlike the pictures my children used to draw—people, places, and things—God drew me. God drew my daughter. He drew my husband's mother, too.

God created us in His own image. He drew us all. And He can be trusted with the memory of the most painful time in our lives. He loves so well. He loves with an everlasting love.

Father God, in days of old You created us in Your own image. You drew us all. You love us so well and we thank You.

Suggested Prayer Topics

*P*ray to know and trust the One who drew you, knows you, and is always with you. For those crushed in spirit. For parents with adult children.

Moving Again!

Dale Witkowski

"But those who hope in the Lord will renew their strength. They will soar on wings like eagles; they will run and not grow weary, they will walk and not be faint." Isaiah 40:31 NIV

Like many people, I lived life one moment at a time, pushing forward no matter the highs or the lows. Knowing the forgiveness of God because of Christ's sacrifice filled me with praise. Six years had passed since I had given the guilt of my sin to the Lord and felt the lightness of burdens lifted. At that time, I was determined to live a life honoring Christ no matter what circumstances surrounded me. Now circumstances weighed heavy on my heart.

My husband changed jobs often, not just within one area, but across states. We finally had our own home with a huge yard bordered by trees and a brook. The community park, bank, church, and stores were all within walking distance. I painted the outside of our home with my favorite blue. My dad and brother put on a new roof. This was home. Our children were now six and one.

Then it happened again. My husband changed jobs, relocating to another state. How could I leave? We would be renters again. I couldn't even pick the place we would move to. My husband did that—a house in the center of a city, with a landlord who didn't really like children. There would be no garden or community park by a lake. My dream of raising my children in our own home with a large yard for play lay destroyed. It would be farther away from family again, too. My heart ached. Anxiety consumed my mind.

Before moving to this new city, I spent a few days at my parent's home. One night during the visit, Eric, my one year old, awoke desiring a bottle. I gathered him up in my arms and went to the living room. It was cold. Exhaustion filled my being. So, I lay down on the rug by the heating vent and cradled Eric in a blanket by my side. Tears began to stream down my face. What will life be like in the rented house in a new city? How can I leave everything behind? There was no going back. Our home was sold.

Silently, I prayed, Lord, help me accept this change. I am so tired and depressed. I don't want to move. What will happen to Deanna? The schools aren't as good. Our daughter, Deanna, was gifted intellectually, and we had worked with the current school to meet her needs. Now we would be moving. More tears crossed my cheeks and dampened my robe.

Suddenly there was a blue light directly across from my position on the rug. A hand was reaching out from the light. At first, I was hesitant. But then I stretched my hand toward the hand that was reaching out to me. A peace without understanding enveloped my body and my baby son. Even though no words were spoken, I knew this was a gift from my Lord. I was His child and He was comforting me. Everything would be all right.

Verses came into my heart and mind. "Every good gift and every perfect gift is from above, and cometh down from the Father of lights, with whom there is no variableness, neither shadow of turning" (James 1:17 KJV). "Who shall separate us from the love of Christ? shall tribulation, or distress, or persecution, or famine, or nakedness, or peril, or sword?... Nay, in all these things we are more than conquerors through him that loved us" (Romans 8:35, 37 KJV). I don't know if the hand reaching out to me was God's hand or Jesus' hand or the hand of an angel sent to comfort me. But it was the love of God surrounding me and lifting me from my depression. My burden was given to the Lord, and I had renewed strength to face another move.

When we settled into that house in the middle of a city, my eyes were open to new blessings. The house was large. My children each had their own bedrooms. The yard was small, but there were lots of flowers. A fantastic church was within walking distance. I was able to sing in the choir, do church musicals, and write Sunday school curriculum. A library with one floor dedicated to children was also within walking distance. The landlord never visited us, so it felt like our own home.

Deanna's school wasn't the best for her. However, the instrumental teacher was phenomenal. Deanna excelled in music. Her love of books and math could not be lessened by the school's placement policy. Again, we were home, despite the new location.

We would move again in a year, and three more times before Deanna and Eric graduated from high school. I miss things in each of our homes but found new blessings in every community. God's loving gift of peace gave me strength to face each and every life challenge. The Holy Spirit ministered to my spirit with love, reminding me constantly of God's promise, "I will never leave you or forsake you" (Hebrews 13:5b NKJV).

Soaring on eagle's wings or not growing weary when running doesn't refer to physical abilities, but spiritual health. There are no circumstances that can steal the love and peace given by the Lord to those who believe in Christ Jesus.

Suggested Prayer Topics

Pray for families separated due to job requirements. Pray for families in transition.

Seekers are Treasures in Abba's Heart

Deb Wuethrich

"Do not fear, for I have redeemed you; I have sum-moned you by name; you are mine." Isaiah 43:1b NIV

I n the Bible, many people ran back to God after a time of big trouble. Their faith waned while trying to do things in their own strength rather than depending on God. I believe God drew me back to Abba's heart after just such a time in my own life.

Our only child, Michele, had a form of muscular dystrophy for which there is no cure. She lived her life at full speed and advocated for people with disabilities. We shared eleven wonderful years before God called her home.

After our loss, my faith spiraled downward even though I was a Christian since youth. When you lose the joy of your life, it's hard to move from the terrible sense of loss and grief to a real trust that this is God's plan.

I still believed but felt spiritually dry, my prayers lifeless and ineffective. I slept in on Sundays instead of going to church. We had Bibles in the house, but I rarely opened them. It wasn't that I didn't know God, but like those folks in the biblical accounts, I was counting on myself alone because (dare I say it?) I felt God had let me down. My journals show a few attempts at seeking, but also questioning God.

When terrorists struck on September 11, 2001, it hit me hard. I was hardly alone. Others, through testimonies, acknowledged this shook them to the core, initiating new searches for God and His will. Ultimately, some returned to faith.

The effects of the attacks were palpable to me. The shock lingered. I can look back and see this horror as a traumatic experience, even though I wasn't present in New York City, Washington, DC, or Shanksville, Pennsylvania. For some, such events can trigger post-traumatic stress, which I experienced. However, it didn't occur to me to see a counselor. I just tried to go on as if nothing had changed when, in many ways, everything had. Deep inside, I wondered, "Where was God?" The thought reverberated off a wall of questions I never dared speak, hearkening back to at least one other time—at Michele's death.

I don't remember a conscious thought that brought it about, but in the early days post-9/11, I did something very unlike me. Each day, I reported to work for a long-term but temporary assignment at City Hall. I packed my tote, tucking in a rarely used Living Bible. During breaks, I took it out and began reading Psalms.

Sitting on a couch in the restroom during morning and afternoon breaks, I didn't care if anyone saw me when this might previously have made me uncomfortable. One day, a co-worker commented it was refreshing to see someone openly reading a Bible. I felt like a hypocrite because it was new for me.

During lunch, I read while eating my sandwich in a conference room. Soon, I couldn't help highlighting and underlining what I found to be amazing passages. They were amazing because I'd never noticed how the psalm writer faced danger, enemies, and fear, like I was feeling. They didn't hesitate to cry to God about it.

I wanted to cry to someone, too! I wanted to believe someone would not only hear but provide answers to the distress!

When underlining was not enough, I filled a notebook with page after page of psalms that brought special comfort or revealed truth I'd never considered. I glimpsed answers to questions I'd stockpiled in my heart.

Soon, I couldn't wait for breaks so I could search God's Word. A Christian told me when we search like that, it's like God is right beside us, revealing His own mind and heart, as well as offering hope. I read at home as well. I couldn't get enough.

Even with emerging faith and a jump-start to a youthful one, you can still miss something: relationship with Jesus Christ. A lot of years poured through my hourglass before I learned such a relationship is possible.

My psalm marathons turned out to be just the beginning of a spiritual awakening. Like the biblical characters, I turned back during a time of crisis. Like many of them, I found having enduring faith can be difficult. Life was to bring other storms and trials and attempts to go my own way.

When the enemy tried to take advantage of my wavering, I chased after some unspiritual things and false teachings, much like my biblical counterparts. Through those times, the psalms stayed with me. Faithful Abba again met me in His Word.

One night, I saw all my past mistakes for what they were: sin. I cried heart-wrenching sobs. Just before falling asleep, I sensed an arm in a white sleeve encircling me. My spirit heard,

"Come to Me." Faith became more than a belief. It became a relationship with Jesus.

One dark night after a meeting, I had a question for Jesus during my drive home.

"How can you put up with someone so fickle in faith?" I asked.

The answer rushed into my heart with lightning speed: "Because you are Mine!" Isaiah 43:1 later mirrored the thought, bringing confirmation. It said, "Do not fear, for I have redeemed you; I have summoned you by name; you are mine" (NIV). The experience strengthened me on this journey back to Him.

After the astounding declaration, in what sounded like a whisper, I heard, "I saw you."

As if directed, my mind raced to when I was reading the book of Psalms every day. God then left this impression: "Did you think I would forget a child so fervently seeking Me?"

Think of a time you felt spiritually dry. Can you remember even one blessing that came from within this period? Was God teaching you to wait? Be patient? To trust? Remember, in calm or trial, you are His!

When we seek God and trust for an answer, we become treasures in Abba's heart. His faithful response assured me I am His forever.

Suggested Prayer Topics

Those who struggle to find hope and to sense God's Presence. (Read Isaiah 43:2–5, verses that follow God's declaration that we are His, and note other affirmations.)

Who Am I?

Mary Burkey

"He leads the humble in what is right, and teaches the humble his way." Psalm 25:9 ESV

God, show me humility," I prayed one day.

He did and is still teaching me.

He answered my prayer in a way I never would have imagined. When I was sixty-eight years old, He revealed to me that Aunt Mary was actually my mother and that her brother and his wife, my aunt and uncle, raised me as their own.

As I set out on a search to know the truth, I questioned myself as to whether I was trying to prove God's faithfulness. Puzzling situations while growing up began to make sense.

I discovered a document from the 1940 census, when it became publicly available on the internet in April 2012. My name appeared in the household of Mom (Elsie) and Dad (Foster) along with my older brother, Bob. This was not proof of who my biological mother was. If Aunt Mary was my mother, it would have shown me living with her on the farm where she lived in 1940. I would have been sixteen days old at the time the census was taken. I struggled through four days of restlessness, then the Holy Spirit led me to look at the document again. Looking more closely, it revealed a birth date for me as July 1939 and not March 23, 1940, my legal birthday. Eight months of aging happened to me in a nanosecond. There was no mistaking the census taker's handwriting. No writing over the numbers or scribbling. A picture of Mom (Elsie) holding me came to mind. In retrieving the picture from an old album, it revealed Elsie's handwriting on the white border: Mother's Day 1940. I could see I did not look like a seven-week-old baby, but I did look like an eight-month-old. God revealed the truth. All who knew the family secret are now deceased. However, the greatest proof was from God.

After this discovery, sadness and regrets overwhelmed me. If I had only known! My actions and responses to Aunt Mary would have been different when in her company. I would have visited her in the nursing home and attended her funeral. One good thing is that after knowing the truth about my birth mother, more of the love from Mom (Elsie) became evident. Not her child or a blood relative, yet she loved me and always made a point of introducing me as her daughter. She taught me a lot about life. Mom (Elsie) was my aunt and Aunt Mary was my mom. I had two moms who loved me very much.

I have forgiven everyone involved in keeping the family secret and not telling me the truth. I understand why things were done the way they were, even with my maternal grandmother who called me a name when I was four years old and told me I wouldn't amount to anything. She could have been kinder, but ethos is powerful. At that time, single mothers were not to keep and raise their babies. Family secrets are probably the best kept secrets.

The revelation of my birth mother was truly humbling. Most of my life was lived with the attitude, "What about me?" This is a sign of great pride. While growing up I developed ugly self-defenses, played the blame game, and became cynical. All are rooted in pride and fear.

This whole eleven-year journey has been bathed in prayer. I would pray about something and God would reveal the answer. Out of His love, He revealed the truth.

Have you noticed when dealing with an issue that lots of circumstances and people come along to help you?

But one person was missing. My birth father, who would now most likely be deceased. Many said that this might be impossible to discover. I spent several hours on genealogy, searching for the answer. One morning last fall, I prayed, "I cannot find my birth father. Will You help me?" Two days later an unknown name of a first cousin, twice removed, and another name of a third cousin appeared in my DNA matches. I also appeared in their DNA matches. Both wrote to me and asked, "Who are you?" I told them I knew my birth mother but was seeking to know my birth father. They said they would help. The next day they had an answer and sent pictures of a relative over the genealogy site. He looked like the man I had seen from time to time as a child. God answered this prayer quickly.

God is still answering my original prayer about humility. Along the way He has revealed much about people and called others to help give me the answers. His grace has been sufficient. It is not sin that humbles me but grace poured out from God. Humility leads to a true relationship with Jesus. When walking humbly with Him, I see His love, His power, and His glory. I now know who I am.

The real truth of who am I? "For you did not receive the spirit of slavery to fall back into fear, but you have received the Spirit of adoption as sons, by whom we cry, 'Abba Father!'" (Romans 8:15 ESV).

And I add, "I belong to You."

Suggested Prayer Topics

*P*ray for God to reveal your identity as His beloved child. Pray God will reveal His love to those who struggle in accepting His love for them.

The Man in the Green Suit

Billie Joy Langston

"And ye shall seek me, and find me, when ye shall search for me with all your heart." Jeremiah 29:13 KJV

For most of my life, friends and family told me I was a blessed child with potential for a good and privileged life. Early on, I acknowledged the sentiment politely while quickly moving on to another subject. The connotation bothered me because it sounded boastful. After all, my parents were ordinary people with extraordinary standards who loved and believed in God. They just wanted the best Christian life for my sister and me. Back then, I didn't realize I'd have to seek God with all my heart to learn His power to provide any privilege my future holds, to include meeting the man in a green suit.

Like my parents, I am a lifelong Christian, baptized at eight years old, in a rural Baptist church. I vividly remember how I bravely stood in front of the congregation during that church revival in the summer of 1965 to confess my faith in Jesus Christ. This was the moment I first knew Jesus loved me, and also the moment I felt most privileged.

When I left home for college, I had no doubt I would not be dissuaded from my Christian background. Rather, I looked forward to enhancing my knowledge and understanding of theology by honing lessons I'd previously learned in Sunday school and vacation Bible school. As a graduate student in the nation's capital, I thought attending chapel on campus and visiting local churches would be a good start for church fellowship.

Although I enjoyed many Sunday services at various churches, I needed more *Baptism,* as in Southern Baptist preaching, singing, and sometimes stomping. Back in southeastern Virginia, we called it *down home church.* Wherever I landed, I knew I'd find the same God, but I was also searching for God's appointed and anointed ordained pastor who just might be packaged a tad differently.

One sunny afternoon while riding on the G-2 bus to the District's popular Georgetown neighborhood, I noticed Mount Sinai Baptist Church located near the corner of Third and Q Streets, NW. The church's name resonated with me because there was a church with the same name in my hometown. I was taken with the church name and building and attended services the next Sunday.

Arriving on time, I entered the church sanctuary and quickly found a seat on a pew located mid-way of the center aisle. As I looked toward the pulpit, God's presence alongside Reverend David Durham was overwhelmingly apparent. I found the church I was seeking, and Reverend Durham became my honorable pastor, preacher, and spiritual mentor.

It was the heart of God being communicated and explained to the entire congregation that made Mount Sinai and Reverend Durham a one-of-a-kind church experience. Reverend Durham's unique way of applying biblical scripture to the reality of everyday life was masterful. He taught the value of spending quality time with the Lord as a way to know Him better and, as a result, to experience His marvelous love and presence more intimately.

Through his unapologetic teachings, I came to know that God loved me unconditionally no matter what I'd done. I learned that mistakes could turn into fortunes instead of dreaded failure. The critical issues I faced were minuscule compared to the sacrifice Jesus made for me. As my faith and trust increased, I gained confidence to explore new opportunities in a renewed relationship with Christ fueled by reliance on His power and promises.

The teachings of the prophet Jeremiah provide insight into the mind and heart of a faithful servant similar to my pastor. When God's people were exiled for seventy years as captives in Babylon, He gave them hope through expressions of great love, mercy, and peace for their expected end. God loved the Israelites as He loves us today by teaching the practice of seeking Him with our whole heart. In doing so, we are allowed to foster a direct relationship with Him.

In addition to being a trusted, reliable source of theology, Reverend Durham's personality was chock-full of humor and no-nonsense demeanor. It was in this context that I learned about his green suit. During a regular one-hour Sunday sermon, he told the congregation about his arrival in Washington, DC as a young preacher from East Spencer, North Carolina, who owned only one green suit that he'd bought on layaway. In dramatic style, Reverend Durham shared stories of going from church to church in an effort to establish himself within the Washington, DC clergy. With each visit, he wore the green suit, sometimes embellished with different colored shirts and ties to disguise wearing the same suit every Sunday.

If I hadn't taken the G-2 bus to Georgetown on that sunny afternoon during graduate school, I may have turned out quite different than I am today. With God's provision, Reverend David Durham led me to become a born-again Christian, which is a great life changing gift from a preacher once known as the man in the green suit.

Now I understand what it truly means to seek God with all my heart and to find Him. When I diligently and purposefully searched for a Bible-based church of God led by a faithful servant, God led me to the right place at the right time.

Like Jeremiah, I persevered to better understand the gospel of Christ for my salvation. I learned to trust God with His long-term restoration plan for my life. Knowing and loving Christ as my personal Savior gave me the new, God-privileged life I've always wanted. This new life is where I can freely express God's unconditional love in a voice of thanksgiving. My God-privileged life is where I am uniquely made with a calling and purpose to fulfill for His glory.

God's love and personal relationship can be found and enjoyed when we seek Him wholeheartedly!

Suggested Prayer Topics

Ask God to reveal His presence in every situation of your life, to reassure you every day of His omnipotence and endless love.

Learning Through Failure

Donna Keith

"Let them thank the Lord *for his steadfast love, for his wondrous works to the children of man!" Psalm 107:8 ESV*

I had failed, failed to finish out the school year as a music teacher and librarian. By the end of the first semester, I was physically, mentally, and emotionally exhausted and asked to be released from my music responsibilities. The school board released me from both jobs. The summer before, I had found myself wanting to get out more in our new community, to have a purpose beyond my household responsibilities, which were minimal since my husband and I were empty nesters. I had an English education degree, had taught English for a few years at our daughters' Christian school, and thought I'd enjoy volunteering at the Christian elementary school in town. While visiting with the administrator, I learned they needed a librarian one day a week and a music teacher two days a week. Though I didn't have a music degree, I had some vocal and instrumental training in my background, and, after a time of prayer, I offered to do both jobs, trusting God to help me do them well.

Even before school started, I felt overwhelmed. The preparation for both subjects was very time consuming, especially for music. My responsibilities included leading the music during chapel and teaching pre-K through fifth grade. I spent hours on lesson planning, incorporating CDs and YouTube videos of Christian and secular music in my teaching. My music responsibilities also included preparing a Christmas program. The administrator was wonderful and helped me choose a simple play with Christmas carols to be sung between scenes.

As the fall progressed, however, I found myself more and more exhausted. I was spending long hours at the school, conducting play practices before school, helping students with their solo and ensemble work during my lunch break, and going in on my days off to do my lesson planning. For library time, I often checked out books from the public library and scoured the internet for materials to reinforce the concepts I was teaching.

I prayed constantly for strength, wisdom, creativity, patience and joy, all of which seemed to come and go. There were a few challenging students, but mostly, I just felt inadequate. I didn't know enough to do both jobs well, in my opinion, but teaching library skills and reading to the students was much easier for me.

My health began to suffer. I was constantly fighting a cough. My mind would not shut down at night as I contemplated things I needed to do in preparation for the Christmas program and my teaching. Wonderful parent volunteers helped with costumes, props, and the set. I had great support from everyone, but I could not shake the feeling that I was drowning. I cried nearly every day. My poor husband heard my laments often. I had signed a contract and felt I had to fulfill it, but as Christmas neared, I found myself desperate for a way out. As disappointed in myself as I was, I felt I could not go on.

Finally, a few weeks before the Christmas program, I turned in my letter of resignation as the music teacher effective at the end of the second quarter. The board felt it best if I leave the school altogether, which broke my heart. Not only had I disappointed myself, but I had let others down as well—students, parents, and the staff. Teachers counted on music and library time away from students to prepare lesson plans. The night of the Christmas program, which went extremely well, was my last time with students as one of their teachers.

I felt great relief, but also guilt, shame, and deep sadness. Alone in my house, I cried buckets of tears. I felt so unlovable. Why had I put the school in this predicament? Why hadn't I just tried to gut it out for one more semester? Why had I agreed to take on the music position in the first place?

God, in His mercy, never let me go. Timely, comforting words from friends and family and the Bible continued to speak to my heart. I began to look back and see how God had ministered in and through me during my time as the school's music and library teacher. Despite my lack of knowledge and talents, God had helped me teach in a way that brought Him glory and blessed the children and me. And He had helped me lead a Christmas program that totally rocked! To Him be the glory!

Though I had failed to complete my contract, I was not a hopeless failure. God sustained me through the first half of the school year and will see me through the healing that is still taking place in my heart, mind, and body. I miss the children. I still wonder if I could have finished out the school year and been okay. I took on a task that I knew would be challenging and trusted God to help me do it (which He did), but the suffering was also very real. My mind is finite. So is my body. I have limitations. The learning goes on!

Have you failed in a way that brings disappointment, shame, and deep sorrow? Like me, I urge you to throw yourself on the mercy of God who cleanses, renews, and comforts us through His Word and the loving encouragement of other believers. Though questions may remain, we can trust God will keep working in us (Philippians 1:6) and heal our brokenness (Psalm 51:17).

Suggested Prayer Topics

Pray for those in difficult situations, that God would sustain them, give them wisdom, and make His love for them evident every day.

The Lost Ring

Karen O. Allen

"Give all your worries and cares to God, for
he cares about you." 1 Peter 5:7 NLT

Peering into my jewelry chest, I noticed the jade ring from my middle-school days. The color would go perfect with my outfit and since the ring was now more than forty years old, it had a vintage look to it, making it even more attractive. Now too small for my ring finger, I slipped it onto my pinky. Although a bit loose, I decided to wear it anyway. The ring looked nice and brought sentimental joy to my heart as I remembered the day my parents bought it for me.

We were on summer vacation, and Daddy told me to pick out a ring from a jewelry store we had gone into to purchase a necklace for Mother. I didn't own an expensive ring. The few rings I had were costume jewelry or dentist box selections, but these rings encased in glass were 14K gold. I found a delicate oblong jade ring with a filigree border that looked just right on my long piano-playing fingers. Mother and Daddy agreed.

I wore the ring for many years, then set it aside. When I tried it on again, I was disgusted and annoyed it no longer fit. A decade passed. But today I would reestablish its purpose.

The audit at work required me to leave the office to go downstairs. As I flipped through the pages of regulatory documents my ring turned round and round on my little finger. I took it off and laid it alongside a bracelet that kept hitting the desk. I placed them in an obvious spot so I'd be sure to remember to put them back on before leaving.

Three hours elapsed before I noticed my bare finger while typing. However, my bracelet was on my wrist. Odd. Where was my ring? I was sure I didn't leave it at the audit sight. Nonetheless, I retraced my steps, crisscrossing my eyes along the floor. No ring. I examined the desk where I had been sitting. No ring. I returned and scoured my office. No ring. Panic was setting in and then I remembered detouring to the restroom near the hospital cafeteria. I flew down the hall like an Olympic speed-walker. I looked all around the sink where I had washed my hands. I am guilty of sometimes taking off my jewelry to wash my hands but still, no ring. The look on my face must have spelled "distress" as one lady asked if there were something wrong. I explained the problem and she remarked, "Perhaps it came off your finger when you dried your hands." But wouldn't I have felt that?

I returned to my office on the verge of tears. During a routine walk with my coworker, I shared my devastating loss. The words of the lady in the restroom kept ringing in my ears. What if it did come off when I wiped my hands dry? Although it was a long-shot, I had to be sure. After our walk, I beelined it back to the restroom and lifted the almost full trash liner out of the can. Confiscating trash, especially in a hospital, is not the smartest thing to do, but this was my last resort to find my precious jade ring. I was stopped by the Environmental Services employee but refused to relinquish my bag of trash as I sped back to my office. I wanted to check the bag in my office but knew it would have to wait.

On my drive home all I could think about was the lost ring. I prayed and cried, cried and prayed. The ring was one of the few things Daddy had given me that reminded me of him, and now that he was in heaven, it meant all the more. God would have to soothe my troubled heart.

After supper I hurried to the basement where I had left the trash bag. Donned in rubber gloves I began unwadding the paper towels one by one. Nothing. A candy wrapper, a few tissues along with a diaper were amongst the paper towels. My hope for the ring diminished with each empty towel. Only one remained. I heard a chink on top of the trash can. Could it be? My heart beat faster. Lord, only You could make this happen. I unwadded the towel. There it was—my beautiful jade and gold ring. I fell to my knees on the plaid dog bed lying on the basement floor. Head bowed, I lifted my hands in praise. The only words I could muster were, "O God." Sincere and utter praise echoed from my lips over and over. "O God, O God."

I fell in love a little deeper with my Abba Father that day and thanked Him for sending the "lady angel" in the restroom who seeded the thought for me to inspect the trash. God cares about the details of our daily lives: the highs, the lows, the mundane, the extraordinary, the expected, and the unexpected. He understands our emotions and from where they evolve. We don't have to explain ourselves to Him, but we benefit from the intimate conversation. As 1 Peter 5:7 encourages us to do, learning to share our thoughts and our emotions with our Abba Father and seeking His direction and comfort leads to a deeper, more fulfilling relationship.

His love enveloped me that night with joy and empathy as I melted with humility on that basement floor. His love was real and it manifested itself in the shape of a size 6 ring!

Suggested Prayer Topics

Pray that our ears will be open to hear God's subtle promptings and to heed His gentle nudging. Be sensitive to God's use of other people to impact our lives.

Can God Really Love Me Unconditionally?

Kelly F. Barr

"How priceless is your unfailing love, O God! People take refuge in the shadow of your wings." Psalm 36:7 NIV

My parents divorced when I was quite young, and when I was four years old, my father abandoned me. Therefore, I grew up with a stepfather who constantly favored my sister over me because she was his by birth. He also made fun of me when I was an overweight teenager. With these earthly examples as fathers, it was difficult to believe God could love me at all, let alone, love me unconditionally. I always felt like I couldn't measure up, couldn't be good enough. I always missed the mark.

Oh, I had some good times in my life, times when Dad (my stepfather) would do something for me unexpectedly, like when he actually went out to buy a Christmas gift for me.

Usually, he left all the Christmas shopping to Mom.

But I always felt like I had to do more to earn love and acceptance. My family wasn't Christian. My mom became a believer, but she didn't have much support. She took me to church sporadically while I was growing up. Each summer she allowed me to attend Bible school at the church we irregularly attended. That's where I opened my heart to Jesus. I was around nine or ten years old. Unfortunately, no one discipled me, so I wasn't sure what to do to follow through with my new-found faith.

As a teenager, I didn't attend church at all. When I was in ninth grade, my stepfather was injured in an accident that hospitalized him for quite some time and required more than one skin-grafting operation. During that time, the church we hadn't attended in years reached out and provided groceries for us and invited me to attend the youth group. I never did.

However, my mom had taught me to pray every night before I went to sleep, and I have always done that. I've prayed for others and for the needs of my family and myself. I never doubted God was there listening, and I always found comfort in speaking to Him.

My grandmother was the constant example of God's unconditional love in my life. She never had an angry word toward anyone. I didn't have to do anything to earn her love. She always loved me, and I was blessed to spend a lot of time with her.

After I graduated from high school and all my friends went their own way, I felt alone. I also felt like something was missing in my life, and I decided to go back to the only church I had ever known. I attended a single-adults Sunday school class. At first, it was hard for me to attend Sunday school and church regularly, partly because my job required I work some Sundays, but mostly because I hadn't learned that regular church attendance was important. But if I missed a couple of Sundays, the single-adults Sunday school teacher would call me to see how I was doing, and she made sure I knew about the social activities they planned and encouraged me to attend. She encouraged me and accepted me just the way I was, and she helped me learn to be a regular Sunday school and church attender.

God continued to put people in my path who knew Him and loved Him and were willing to show His love to me. They introduced me to contemporary Christian music and invited me to Christian events for young people, including the old Christian coffee houses. He also put a young lady in my life who knew Him and loved Him, and she became my best friend. She invited me to her church and to a huge Christian event that still takes place annually, the Creation Festival. I also went to a lot of contemporary Christian music concerts with her. One that stands out in my mind that also showed me that God knows, accepts, and loves me unconditionally was when we saw Geoff Moore and the Distance two years in a row. The second year, when we spoke with Geoff after the concert, he said he remembered seeing me the year before! I couldn't believe with all of the faces he saw in a year's time that he would remember *my* face.

Eventually, I met and married a young man who had grown up in the church I had learned to attend regularly. We continue to attend and be active in a church to this very day. We've raised our sons to know God's love and the importance of being part of a Bible-teaching church.

Over the years, God has shown me in many ways—some small, some big—that He loves me unconditionally. I would have to say that two of the biggest ways I have seen God's unconditional love is in the way He has answered many of my prayers, and in the way He has revealed to me, as I've reflected on my life, that He has always been with me and guided my steps. If I stumbled from His path, He's always guided me back.

I have no doubt God is real and He loves me even when I stumble and fall. He loves me with an awesome love. He loves me unconditionally.

No matter what you're going through, know that God loves you and He is near. Pray, knowing He is listening. Take refuge in His wings, and you, too, will find His unfailing love.

Suggested Prayer Topics

Ask God to reveal His truth to you. For your faith and trust in God to grow. That God would reveal to you how He's been present and working in your life. That you would come to recognize and accept His love.

Overcome

Nancy Kelley Alvarez

*"Don't let evil conquer you, but conquer evil
by doing good." Romans 12:21 NLT*

My excitement knew no bounds when my husband and I adopted Pete,* an eleven-year-old Filipino boy.

When we discovered we could not have our own children, adoption became our hope. At long last, I enjoyed the reality of motherhood. When, after three years, Pete began running away, disillusionment threatened to crush me, leaving me numb and dazed.

Pete disappeared eleven times in one year. The last time he was gone for a month. In addition, this happened in Manila, a metropolis of twelve million where the police force is spread too thin to track runaway children. And Pete is a slender, brown skinned boy with black hair and eyes—just like millions of other boys his age. How could we ever find him?

Long conversations with the Lord of my life usually began with a host of questions: Where did I go wrong? Why are You allowing this to happen? Didn't I try everything to help Pete? Was I too strict? Not strict enough? The endless questions and accusations still reverberate in my mind. The shame, anger, and disappointment adhere like a thick mud, pushing me to the verge of depression. How I long for a dramatic ending, proving God's great power and love for me, but not much has changed. Although we eventually found him, Pete moved out of the house at sixteen, his empty room a constant reminder of my failure.

Through it all, I did not doubt God's love, yet I couldn't feel it either. I searched His Word for answers. After many months, I came upon Romans 12—a chapter full of practical advice on handling relationships.

"Don't just pretend to love others. Really love them. Hate what is wrong. Hold tightly to what is good. ...Rejoice in our confident hope. Be patient in trouble, and keep on praying. ...Don't let evil conquer you, but conquer evil by doing good (Romans 12:9,12,21 NLT).

Bam! As I sought God's comfort, strength, and wisdom, the last verse came alive. The slippery slope of loss developed into a journey of discovery. Acting on a suggestion, I began devouring books on the oppression that youth and women face today throughout the world. My pain paled in comparison to what many experience.

Despite my son's continued rebellion, the Lord infused me with a desire to turn the pain into good—in other words to conquer and overcome evil with good. While I can't force Pete to live for Jesus, I can bless others experiencing their own stories of sorrow.

I asked the Lord for an opportunity to help oppressed women, especially victims of human trafficking. After much waiting and perseverance, a door opened to volunteer at an organization that hired and rehabilitated sexually exploited victims. I needed to get up at 4:30 a.m. in order to arrive for the weekly 7 a.m. devotional time. As an introvert, I felt way out of my comfort zone. I didn't know if I could build good rapport with the thirty women.

Throughout the four years of visiting, I became deeply committed to the young women as we laughed and cried together, sharing our joys and heartaches. I told stories of women from the Bible—Hagar, Sarah, Esther, and others—who had also experienced cruelty as well as God's love. When I asked the women what they learned from these stories, they said: "Never give up; there's always hope; God loves me; God has a good plan for me." A hallelujah chorus erupted in my heart.

Teaching these women, reaffirmed God's love for me as well. As we struggled together to make sense of our grief, I gained a deeper awareness of God's love and comfort. We studied story after story of His great love for women and children, His intense involvement in their lives, and His mercy and grace for all who put their trust in Him.

I am determined to put Romans 12:21 into practice. As God continues to lead, I won't let discouragement overcome me. With the Lord's help, I will conquer sin with good. He isn't through with me or my son. My fluttering emotions can drag me into despair or tug me closer to Jesus—it's up to me.

I can't control my son's choices, and I don't want his defiance to hold such power over me that I become a useless lump of dirty snow. As I see women around me transformed by God's Word, I gain a little more faith that He can work in the lives of those I love. When I help shoulder others' burdens, joy wraps around me, lifting me above the lies that the evil one uses to taunt me. Although I hope my son will live a godly life someday, meanwhile I can give thanks for the opportunity to comfort others. God still loves me despite my failures, and He makes me a blessing to others.

"He comforts us in all our troubles so that we can comfort others. When they are troubled, we will be able to give them the same comfort God has given us. For the more we suffer for Christ, the more God will shower us with his comfort through Christ." (2 Corinthians 1:4,5)

While I may not have chosen this form of suffering, it's what God has chosen for me. I can either rebel or welcome it.

What disappointments threaten to destroy your faith and assurance of God's love? Perhaps God is speaking to you about a way you could be a comfort to others by overcoming evil with good. What initial step can you take?

Read Romans 12:9–21. Ask God to speak to you about what action He would like you to take. Based on 2 Corinthians 1:3–4, who comes to mind that you could comfort?

Suggested Prayer Topics

Ask the Lord to comfort the hearts of those who are hurting and experiencing loss. Ask the Lord to loudly affirm His love for you and to show you how to overcome evil with good. Listen for His directions.

Name changed to protect privacy.

He Cares for You

Debra L. Butterfield

"And my God shall supply all your need according to His riches in glory by Christ Jesus." Philippians 4:19 NKJV

Tracy, after months of evaluation and prayer, I've decided to quit my job and move to Missouri."

Shock registered on my boss's face at my declaration. Months of seeking direction had yielded no definitive answers. In reality, the desire to leave Colorado had plagued me for the past eleven years. Ever since my husband confessed to sexually abusing my daughter, the comfy home we once shared had become a tomb.

Apprehension stimulated my heart rate to just under cardiac arrest when I gave July 29 as my last day. The Realtor hadn't yet pushed the "For Sale" sign into the front yard. Without a job, how would I pay the bills if the house didn't sell? Did I trust money or God? Had I made the right decision or a giant mistake? My answer volleyed like a tennis ball at Wimbledon.

"How exciting," my co-workers would say. "What new job are

you going to?" Many commented on my faith when they learned I had none. Their comments forced me to examine my faith. The Hebrew patriarch Abraham came to mind. What did he feel when God said leave your country and go to a place I'll show you?

Abraham had a promise and his faith in God. I yearned for life at a slower pace. For less traffic and small-town living, for green grass and all four seasons, all of which Colorado Springs didn't offer. My Midwest childhood home beckoned me.

Three weeks after the Realtor posted her sign, the house sold. I believed this was a confirmation from God.

The last eleven years had been some of the roughest of my life, which included divorce and putting my family back together after my husband's crime and jail time, and reentering the work world after ten years of being a stay-at-home mom. I had a $60,000 profit on my house, and so I decided to take things easy my first year in Missouri. I sought God and what He had for me and wondered about the dreams I still had for my life but not yet realized.

When I started job hunting, I couldn't find one. Some part-time work, but nothing full-time. God kept bringing me back to something a co-worker had said about writing a book. I took the plunge and started writing. In 2007, I published my first book. I was on my way to realizing my dream as a writer.

Book sales were slow to non-existent. I didn't know how to market my book. I started a blog and kept looking for work. Was I truly trusting God to provide? I frequently quoted Philippians 4:19, "And my God shall supply all your need according to His riches in glory by Christ Jesus" (NKJV). My faith wavered, a lot.

In early 2010, things came to a head. My $60K profit had long ago been consumed. Part-time jobs had helped, but I needed a steady way to pay the bills.

The job market was dismal at best, the economy only beginning to recover from the 2008 recession. As I sat one morning reading my Bible and praying, I cried out to God. "I'm so tired of constantly battling with money all the time. God, you've got to do something." I questioned myself, probably for the thousandth time, whether moving to Missouri had been God's plan for me. I cried for several minutes, then finished praying. I told God I knew He would take care of me.

My mom had requested I come over that morning and had asked my siblings from out of town to be there also. My father had died a few months earlier and there were still things to settle, so this didn't seem like anything strange.

After we were all there, my mom explained that now she was the last remaining beneficiary of my grandmother's trust fund, she had decided to dissolve it. This was actually not to occur until my mother died. She and my brother had been working for several weeks with the necessary people to make it happen.

She handed each of us a check. I took mine and said thank you, but did not immediately look at the amount. I started to protest that she had done this, but she quickly cut me off.

"I wanted to do this for each of you. I know several of you have been struggling financially," she said.

At that point, I looked down at the check written in the amount of $93,000. (My three siblings got a check for the same amount.) Tears immediately sprang to my eyes, and I started crying. God had answered my prayer and in less than four hours! But He had been preparing that answer long before I expressed my need. That's often how He works in our lives.

God strengthened my faith that morning, and I have reminded myself of that extravagant provision many times when other difficulties assaulted me.

God loves His children. He generously provides all we need so we can share with others (2 Corinthians 9:8). He delights in our prosperity (Psalm 35:27). We can trust His Word. "God is not a man, so he does not lie. He is not human, so he does not change his mind. Has he ever spoken and failed to act? Has he ever promised and not carried it through?" (Numbers 23:19 NLT).

Suggested Prayer Topics

Ask the Lord to reveal any lies you might believe about His desire to bless you. Ask Him how you might be a blessing to someone in your life.

Here's Your Sign

Gina Napoli

*"Then the LORD replied: 'Write down the revelation
and make it plain on tablets so that a herald
may run with it.'" Habakkuk 2:2 NIV*

When God tries to get my attention, He sends the Holy Spirit to clunk me on the head. He has to.

I especially felt that clunk a few years ago.

My daughter had been having a string of bad days—a string long enough to send a kite to the moon. I had been praying, but God didn't offer me solace quickly enough. Her grades weren't great; the teachers emailed me constantly; and she couldn't keep friendships.

Her bad days felt heightened by a recent ADHD diagnosis. Her extremes in behavior impacted the whole family. If everything in her day progressed perfectly or held the absence of anything rotten, then we enjoyed peace. If one teeny-tiny piece of her world's minutiae was askew, then everything in her life felt unsalvageable to her.

I enrolled her in after-school activities, thinking it would help. If I knew about the grueling commute, I would have hosted the chess club, basketball team, choir, Legion of Mary, and Girl Scouts at my house. As summer approached, more cars clogged the roadways through the most touristy parts of Hershey, Pennsylvania, with its sprawling amusement park, indoor and outdoor amphitheaters, and a chocolate factory slightly less clandestine than Willie Wonka's. (Hershey did acquire some Wonka products. Maybe the Oompa Loompas commuting from Loompa-Land caused increased traffic?)

I took a different route one particular day, thinking I could outsmart the other commuters. Nope.

My long commute felt like an excellent time to pray, at least until some orange-skinned, green-haired driver cut me off. I tried mustering my patience, although I didn't always lead with that. My baby wasn't thriving, and the Lord wasn't working fast enough to grow her.

This particular stretch of highway was a known must-to-avoid, complete with weird six-point intersections and flow-interrupting traffic lights. I didn't know what I was thinking driving this way. I didn't want this extra time, even to pray and finish my coffee. I needed to know how my daughter's day went before my own life could feel right. I needed the full report so I could rejoice or commiserate with her, and tell her she would forget about her childhood nonsense until her own children went through it.

"Lord? Are you there?" I sipped my coffee. "Lord?"

I counted the stick figures on the rear window of the minivan in front of me. I wondered how these parents managed with four girls. Just one felt like plenty to me.

I looked at the sky through my windshield. "Lord, if You're everywhere, then You're here. Even right here in the middle of hell."

I glanced to my left and saw a black billboard with white

lettering that read: WE NEED TO TALK. –GOD

Whoa. I gripped the wheel. "That was kinda creepy," I said to no one in the passenger seat, placing the coffee in the cup-holder between us.

Well, since He brought it up…

"Lord? I don't know what I'm doing. I'm trying my hardest, but I still feel like a lousy mother."

The next billboard read: DETERMINATION, with the second "T" branded for Temple University. The billboard next to it read: MAKING A DIFFERENCE FOR GENERATIONS. Some public service announcement. But still, weirdly on the nose.

"Lord, I know I can't sit with her at lunch or shield her from every bully. But if I can't protect her, then who will?"

The next billboard brought another public service announcement: PROTECT PA FAMILIES. Beside it was another billboard for a home improvement company called CHAMPION.

Wow, it even used the word *protect*. Had I seen the billboard out of the corner of my eye before asking the question?

"I feel like we're on a hamster wheel. I don't feel we're growing as a family."

The next billboard, this one from a local landscaping company, read: LET'S GARDEN TOGETHER. A family patted the earth around a tree, leaning on garden equipment.

Was I reading what I wanted to interpret, or was the Holy Spirit speaking to me through Lamar Advertising?

"Lord, if You're really talking to me, will our family ever get through this? What's our path?"

I swear I'm not making this up. Two companies each bought half a billboard. One side was for a spa called DOLCE, which means "sweet," and the other was for a store named JOURNEYS. The Lord wanted to tell me we would have sweet journeys. Journeys even added the advice: SHAKE UP YOUR STYLE.

Billboards and prayers fresh in my mind, I reached the parking lot of my daughter's school. I braced myself. "Lord, good day, please?" I prayed. As she walked toward my car, I tried to read her face for any micro-expression to give me a clue how our house would be that night.

"How was school?" I tried to sound bright.

She wouldn't answer at first. Her delay left me perched on a ledge, trying to surmise clues like an amateur detective.

Finally, she said, "That's hard to answer today. It wasn't all good. It wasn't all bad. A few annoying things happened, but they didn't spoil the whole day."

Driving the opposite way down that same stretch of road, I read the Holy Spirit's final telling billboard: Wellspan Health Network asked: WHAT'S YOUR BREATHTAKING MOMENT?

Wherever Wellspan was going with that question, I didn't know. But I had no doubt that the Holy Spirit brought me God's message through each billboard. It doesn't get any clearer than the Holy Spirit clunking a person on the head with an enormous literal sign.

My experience reminded me of the Bible verse called "The Lord's Answer" in Habakkuk 2:2: "Then the LORD replied: Write down the revelation and make it plain on tablets so that a herald may run with it" (NIV).

My prayer for us all is that when God speaks to us, we may know it in our hearts, and then proclaim it to all, serving as a sign that God loves us.

Suggested Prayer Topics

*P*ray for those with mental illness and behavioral disorders.

Contributors

KAREN O'KELLEY ALLEN recently retired from working in cancer research. A diagnosis of breast cancer inspired her to write her Bible study *Confronting Cancer with Faith*, which has brought encouragement and hope around the world. Her Ewe R Blessed blog highlights everyday and unexpected blessings through life's trials. — confrontingcancerwithfaith.com

NANCY ALVAREZ writes stories that inspire risk-taking faith and courage, making a positive difference in the world one person at a time through the love of Jesus. She's passionate about empowering women to thrive in today's challenging world. She lives in the Philippines with her husband and part-dog part-angel Bingo. She is the author of *The Butterfly Impact* and *The Opportunity*, found on Amazon.com.

KELLY F. BARR lives in Lancaster County, Pennsylvania, with her husband and youngest son. She is a skilled freelance writer and editor, as well as a blogger. She is a member of Lancaster Christian Writers. She is currently revising her first historical romance that she hopes will be published within the next year or so. In her free time, she enjoys taking walks with her black Labrador Retriever.

CATHERINE ULRICH BRAKEFIELD is an ardent lover of Christ, as well as a hopeless romantic and patriot. She skillfully intertwines these elements into her novels, Wilted Dandelions and the Destiny series. Catherine enjoys horseback riding, swimming, camping, and traveling the byroads across America with Edward, her husband of fifty years.
—CatherineUlrichBrakefield.com

MARY LOUISE BURKEY is a wife, mother, and grandmother. She wrote *Broken Branch*, a memoir of a life journey that was guided by a family secret never to be divulged. God does not keep secrets. In His perfect timing, He revealed the truth and it drew her closer to Him. She has learned to seek God's help. He answers and teaches her more about Him.

DEBRA L. BUTTERFIELD is an author, conference speaker, and editorial director of CrossRiver Media Group. She also works as a freelance editor and is currently writing her first novel. She blogs about the craft of writing at TheMotivationalEditor.com. You can find her author blog at DebraLButterfield.com. Debra is a Marine Corps veteran and has three adult children and two grandchildren.

LINDA RAY CENTER is a blogger, motivational speaker, and a relationship builder. She retired from a thirty-two-year career in dance education. Linda and her husband reside in the Deep South, and she treasures her relationships with family, friends, and kids. She is a hands-on grandmother and will showcase her grandchildren's pictures at any given time.

ABBA'S ANSWERS

DR. JEANETTA CHRYSTIE is a freelance writer and speaker in Springfield, Missouri. Her published writing includes more than 800 magazine articles, 150+ newspaper columns, many devotions, and poems. Jeanetta is an adjunct faculty member for Southwest Minnesota State University and Judson University in Illinois. — ClearGlassView.com.

NANCY ENNA COWART is a pen name for a writer from the Deep South.

DOROTHY DOSWALD didn't fall in love with literature until her first semester in college, and then the dam broke and books flooded her life. She went into education, focusing on the early years so she could teach her students to read. With a forty-year marriage, two grown kids, and five rascally grandkids, her life is full. She has written for her own children, her students, and her church.

CAROLYN FISHER is the author of *When You Can't, God Can*, a memoir of how God saved her marriage, and *The Tea Set*, a Christian romance. Her poetry has been published in *Maturity Magazine* and EA Publishing's *Blessings in Disguise*.

BARBARA GORDON is a former school teacher and administrator who began freelance writing after retirement. She writes nonfiction and has been published in *The Secret Place, Seek, The Upper Room, Keys for Kids, Breakthrough Intercessor,* and *Live.* She has also had devotions printed in numerous anthology books. Barbara enjoys traveling and family time.

GAIL GRITTS has been a missionary in England for over thirty-five years. She has traveled the world, lost her passport in China, ridden an elephant, and raised five wonderful children. Gail is a freelance writer and speaker and writes *Beside the Well,* ggritts.blogspot.com. She is the author of the Reba and Katherine children's book series. —GailGritts.com

MOLLY WOODS is a nurse who loves to write, read, and create. She is a recovering addict, nearly a decade clean and actively working her recovery program, which includes sponsoring other women. She lives in Spokane, Washington, with her husband, James, and has two adult children. Molly loves the Lord, believes all life experiences are useful, and that God wastes absolutely nothing.

CHERYL J. HESER is a former teacher and longtime director of Rosebud County Library in Forsyth, Montana. She was honored by the Montana Library Association as the 2014 Librarian of the Year. After retirement, she earned an MFA in Creative Writing from Lindenwood University. She is also a wife, mother, doting grandmother, pianist, active church member, hiker, and photographer.

Since the age of nine, LINDA HIGHMAN has accepted the claims of Christ on her life. One claim was graduating from Bob Jones University where she met her husband in the radio choir. Another was teaching at the same Christian schools with him for twenty-seven years. They have made their home in her native Portland, Oregon, for the past thirty-eight years.

DONNA KEITH is a wife, mother, and grandmother of six. She has a BS in English Education, and taught junior and senior high school English as well as English to internationals in her community. She has four published children's books with more to come. Donna loves to spend time with her family, play golf, walk, travel with her husband, Lee, and serve others through ministry opportunities.

Queen of Fun and Coffee Cup Philosopher CATHY KRAFVE puts a snappy spin on deeply spiritual truths. As a columnist, blogger, podcaster, speaker, and small business owner, Cathy understands life is about companionship. She desires to create life so beautiful in its imperfection that generations after us will be retelling our stories with joy and laughter. Truth with a Texas twang spoken here!

DEEDEE LAKE, The Connection Expert, speaker, author, blogger, and columnist, builds relationships one conversation at a time using humor, storytelling, and purposeful communication. As owner of Cherish Relations Retreats, she lives out her faith and passion while writing, speaking, and guiding individuals how to have extraordinary relationships. She and husband, Seth celebrated their thirty-eighth wedding anniversary.

DEBRA L. BUTTERFIELD

BILLIE JOY LANGSTON is a journalist and freelance writer of inspirational and positive living literature. Her publishing credits include anthologies in two Guideposts books, *Miracles Do Happen* (2019) and *In the Arms of Angels* (2021), in addition to *Chicken Soup for the Soul – I'm Speaking Now* (2021). Billie enjoys spending leisure time at east and west coast beaches with her feet buried in fluffy, flour-like sand.

NORMA C. MEZOE has been a published writer for thirty-four years. Her writing has appeared in books, devotionals, take-home papers, and magazines. She is a regular contributor to Christiandevotions.us. She is active in her church in a variety of roles. Norma may be contacted at normacm@tds.net

GINA NAPOLI is a writer, full-time mom, Christian, lifelong learner. She is the author of the book *Clunk on the Head: How the Holy Spirit Got Our Attention,* a collection of twenty-eight stories from twelve authors who have had direct interaction with the Holy Spirit.

CAROL ROUND is the author of nine books, including three collections of her columns, a book and companion workbook on prayer journaling, and a three-book series for children to teach them the importance of giving, saving, and spending their money. Her book *Growing Confidently in Your Faith* is a fifty-two-week devotional/spiritual journal to help women draw closer to the Lord.

BARBARA VILLARREAL is a mother of four grown children and ten amazing grandchildren, and lives in southern Alabama with her two Siamese cats, Lovey and Cuddles. She enjoys writing speculative Christian fiction for children and adults. She spends time with her family and enjoys all that nature has to offer.

Born in California, DEBBIE JONES WARREN moved to Nigeria with missionary parents before her first birthday. Beginning at age six, she lived in a boarding school eight months per year. Now she's writing her stories, seeking to find God in the difficult journey. She and her husband, Chris, live in Castro Valley. — debbiejoneswarren.com

DALE WITKOWSKI is an artist, art teacher, sanctuary steward, and mission director at her church. The Lord has blessed her with six children. Dale retired from teaching in 2019 and commits time each day to sharing all the Lord has done in her life.

DEB WUETHRICH is a retired newspaper staff writer, living in Portville, New York. Her work has appeared in several anthologies, magazines, and a weekly column, "Home Again," appears in the *Olean Times Herald*. Deb also leads Southern Tier Christian Writers of Olean, New York.

DONNA WYLAND is an award-winning author, editor, and coach. Her work has appeared in numerous publications. Author of picture books, *Your Home in Heaven* and *If I Could Ask Jesus*, and the newly released gift book, *Surrender*, Donna's work encourages readers to draw near to God as they anticipate eternity with Him. Connect with Donna on Instagram (@ *freetobe_writer_coach*) and Pinterest. — freetobe.faith

Discover more great books from…
CrossRiverMedia.com

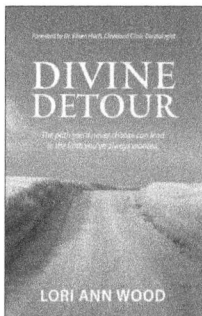

Divine Detour

A serious medical diagnosis took Lori Ann Wood on a faith detour she never saw coming. As a believer, she was profoundly disappointment in the God she thought she knew. *Divine Detour* is the result of Lori Ann's risky decision to embrace difficult questions. Join her on a forty-day journey deep into the heart of a God who often doesn't behave as we'd like. You'll learn to embrace the questions everyone encounters so your faith can thrive during your own inevitable detour.

An Unnatural Beauty

Holiness is not an endless list of "thou shalt nots." It's not how we behave, what we think, or how we react or respond to life and the people around us. You'll discover foundational truths from Scripture, the path to a deeper, more intimate relationship with God, and why holiness can't be achieved through our own efforts. Esther reminds us that Holiness is not a what, but a glorious Who, and He's inviting you to share in His divine nature.

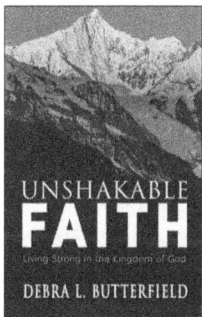

Unshakable Faith

With *Unshakable Faith*, you'll build an indestructible foundation to your faith and crush your doubts. This 7-week Bible study contains lessons designed to be completed in 20 minutes or less. Topics covered include your kingdom identity, faith fundamentals, your authority and power, and your weapons and armor. You'll grow and strengthen your faith, learn faith fundamentals, and learn to command the power and authority God has given you.

Answers, gifts, lessons love and promises...

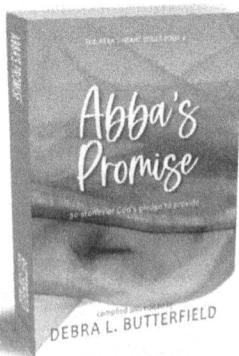

Abba's Answers
compiled by DEBRA L. BUTTERFIELD

Abba's Gifts
compiled by TAMARA CLYMER

Abba's Heart
compiled by TAMARA CLYMER

Abba's Lessons
compiled by DEE DEE LAKE

Abba's Promise
compiled by DEBRA L. BUTTERFIELD

Abba's Devotion series

Available in bookstores and online retailers.

Even more great books from…
CrossRiverMedia.com

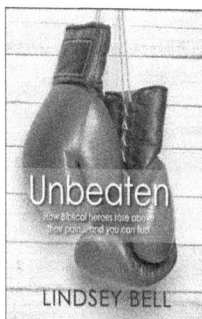

Unbeaten

Difficult times often leave us searching the Bible for answers to the most difficult questions—Does God hear me when I pray? Why isn't He doing anything? Author Lindsey Bell understands the struggle. As she searched the Bible for answers to these tough questions, her studies led her through the stories of biblical figures. She discovered that while life brings trials, faith brings victory. And when we rely on God for the strength to get us through, we can emerge *Unbeaten*.

Big Steps Little Steps

Life can feel chaotic, but *Big Steps, Little Steps* is a devotional that meets you wherever you are. No dates, no pressure—open it anytime for encouragement. Discover 12 weeks of practical insights that address everyday struggles, applying Scripture to real life. Ideal for daily devotions—no falling behind. Whether your steps are giant leaps or tentative tiptoes, God promises to guide you forward. Grab your copy today!

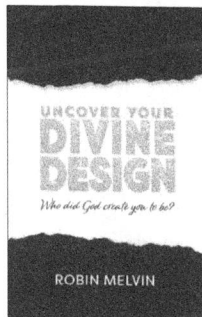

Uncover Your Divine Design

Tired of toxic thoughts and feeling like you'll never measure up? *Uncover Your Divine Design* helps you embrace your true identity in Christ. Through personal stories, scripture, and practical steps, Robin Melvin reveals how to uncover lies, heal past wounds, and live in God's love. Learn to see yourself as God does—worthy, whole, and wonderfully His. Step into the abundant life you were created for.

Books that build
battle-ready faith.

If you enjoyed this book, will you consider sharing it with others?

- Please mention the book on Facebook, Instagram, Pinterest, or your blog.

- Recommend this book to your small group, book club, and workplace.

- Head over to Facebook.com/CrossRiverMedia, 'Like' the page and post a comment as to what you enjoyed the most.

- Pick up a copy for someone you know who would be challenged or encouraged by this message.

- Write a review on your favorite online book platform.

- To learn about our latest releases subscribe to our newsletter at CrossRiverMedia.com.

www.ingramcontent.com/pod-product-compliance
Lightning Source LLC
Chambersburg PA
CBHW060209070426
42447CB00035B/2877